International Management Leadership
The Primary Competitive Advantage

INTERNATIONAL BUSINESS PRESS
Erdener Kaynak, PhD
Executive Editor

New, Recent, and Forthcoming Titles:

International Management Leadership
The Primary Competitive Advantage

Raimo W. Nurmi, PhD
John R. Darling, PhD

International Business Press
An Imprint of The Haworth Press, Inc.
New York • London

Published by

International Business Press, an imprint of The Haworth Press, Inc., 10 Alice Street, Binghamton, NY 13904-1580

Cover design by Marylouise E. Doyle.

Library of Congress Cataloging-in-Publication Data

Nurmi, Raimo.
    International management leadership : the primary competitive advantage / Raimo W. Nurmi, John R. Darling.
      p.   cm.
    Includes bibliographical references and index.
    ISBN 0-7890-0260-4 (alk. paper).
    1. Industrial management. 2. Leadership. I. Darling, John R. II. Title.
HD31.N86 1997
658.4′092–dc21
                                      97-2108
                                        CIP

CONTENTS

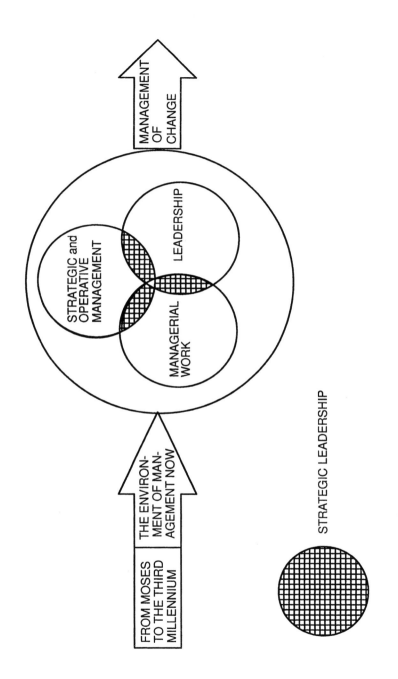

MANAGEMENT OF CHANGE

LEADERSHIP

STRATEGIC and OPERATIVE MANAGEMENT

MANAGERIAL WORK

THE ENVIRON-MENT OF MAN-AGEMENT NOW

FROM MOSES TO THE THIRD MILLENNIUM

STRATEGIC LEADERSHIP

ABOUT THE AUTHORS

Raimo Nurmi, PhD, is Professor of Business Administration at the Turku School of Economics and Business Administration in Turku, Finland, where he has taught for almost 25 years. Dr. Nurmi has worked for a variety of organizations around the world, including: Oy Mec-Rastor Ab (the Finnish unit of the International H.B. Maynard Management Consulting Company); the International Labour Organization's Centre for Management Development in Lagos, Nigeria; the Food and Agricultural Organization's West African Centre for Agricultural Credit Training in Freetown, Sierra Leone; and the Deakin University School of Management in Victoria, Australia. Dr. Nurmi has published a number of books and articles on management, leadership, organization, and cross-cultural subjects.

John R. Darling, PhD, is President of Pittsburg State University in Pittsburg, Kansas, where he is also Professor of International Business. Previously, Dr. Darling was Chancellor and Distinguished Professor of International Business at Louisiana State University in Shreveport; he has also held teaching and leadership positions at several other universities in the United States, and visiting professorships at various universities in Taiwan, Mexico, Bulgaria, Australia, Poland, Estonia, Egypt, South Korea, and Japan. Dr. Darling regularly travels to Finland as Visiting Distinguished Professor of International Marketing at the Helsinki School of Economics. He is the author or co-author of several books, monographs, and numerous articles published in academic and professional journals. He has also been a consultant to many U.S. and foreign businesses and organizations.

Preface

There was once a sculptor who had carved a singular statue from a huge block of stone. A passerby asked what the statue represented, and the response was, "It is the statue of Opportunity." "But why," asked the passerby, "do you have the statue standing on its toes?" "Because Opportunity stays but a moment," the sculptor answered. "Then why do you have wings on its ankles?" "Because Opportunity flies quickly," was the reply. "Why do you have a lock of hair on its forehead?" The sculptor paused for a moment and replied, "When Opportunity approaches, you can seize it easily." "Why then do you have a bald place on the back of its head?" "When Opportunity passes by, you cannot seize it," the sculptor concluded.

One of the primary secrets of success in international management leadership is for an individual to be ready for an opportunity when it arises. Reacting responsibly to the opportunities for development and serving as a catalyst for helping to create such opportunities within international organizations are two key roles for the managerial leader today. Yet to fulfill these roles requires the courage to live with uncertainty.

Each day brings its own opportunities, its own issues, and requirements for decision-making. The conditions within which the international managerial leader must function are not altogether controllable, predictable, safe, or certain. Courage must be acquired to live and creatively interact in an environment as it is, not only as it may be desired. Courage has been considered to be one of the greatest of all virtues, because if one does not have courage, one may not have an opportunity to use any of the others.

Today is truly an exciting period of time in international business affairs. All around are heard the drumbeats of opportunities and problems relating to technology, productivity, government, international relations, social values, health care, human relations, etc. This day offers, as no other day in recorded human history, advantages for business relations and for business leaders who can properly identify the problems which are evolving and translate these into meaningful opportunities for organizational achievement. However, taking hold of a problem/opportunity is often made easier if it is approached with a one-at-a-time perspective. One step—a beginning—doing something about the issue, beginning to see accomplishment—gives assurance that the journey has begun, and the achievement of objectives is possible. In international management leadership, as in all other professional fields, success is a progressive journey and not a final destination. In directing organizational activities, the managerial leader must select what is important, what is possible, and move from where the organization is with the foundation that has been established.

With this orientation for the future, a certain creatively disciplined power, which may be called the "Spirit of Achievement," will become reflected in international managerial leaders. It is a perspective that will continue to call individuals forth to the fulfillment of purposes and the realization of goals. Once acquired and developed, this Spirit will prevent managerial leaders from mistaking a temporary setback for a permanent defeat, readily acknowledging an obstacle to be insurmountable, or being at the end of one's creative resources when conventional methods fail. In perspective, managerial leaders see goal achievement as a practical possibility, know there is some way to accomplish legitimate expectations, and are ready to create new measures when old measures fail. Such a Spirit must be a reflected reality in international managers if they are to play a meaningful role in the continued growth and development of the organizations they are called upon to lead.

Managerial leaders in international corporations and other organizations have discovered an interesting trend in recent years. It is hard to pick up a professional or business magazine or journal, attend a professional meeting, or have a discussion with one's staff, peers or superiors, without the concept of leadership emerging as a primary topic of interest and concern. We are all called upon to exert an influence on those about us; in other words, to be a leader. As professionals, we have read or been involved in one discussion or another where we examine the question of leadership. Our reading or discussions invariably introduce concepts that describe what constitutes leadership characteristics, management styles, individual versus organizational goals, conflict resolution procedures, problem-solving techniques, and recognized models of management.

In the final analysis, although we can conceptualize, theorize, analyze, and dissect all the parts to describe them in detail, then reconstruct them into a gestalt to see the whole person working in a system, we still have unexplained questions about what makes someone a successful managerial leader. One thing we can feel secure and justified in assuming, however, is that an individual is exhibiting leadership when his or her own behavior or attitude helps to change, in a positive way, the behavior (attitude or action) of another individual or group of individuals.

This is the particular influence for which managerial leaders are often hired. This attribute is constant in every culture. They are asked to orient themselves toward the objectives and goals of their organization and to lead their fellow managers, staff members, and selected outside publics toward the satisfaction of the superordinate goals. Individual needs, subgroup needs, and the transactions between leaders and followers become paramount in the process of achieving organizational goals and in adapting to the situations or problems of the moment. Problem solving, conflict resolution, and resistiveness to change are always part and parcel of the transactions between a leader and his or her followers.

There are numerous ingredients in both the description and analyzation of management and leadership. The dynamics of this interaction are a constant challenge, and those involved in the managerial leadership of international business firms and other organizations derive a great deal of satisfaction and certainly motivational impetus to actions by the forces involved. The inevitable conflicts among personalities, use of resources, corporate and individual goals, national and international government guidelines, board of directors, and managers and staff create situations and events that demand creativity and imaginative solutions.

In business firms involved in multicultural settings with personnel from different cultures and who speak different languages, this becomes even more critical. It is within this climate of uncertainty and potential conflict that motivational management and leadership characteristics emerge and grow. In analyzing these issues, the authors reached the conclusion that complete organizational unity within the international business firm is probably best described as an often sought after state; however, in actuality is an impossible dream. In further response to the above-noted concept that success is a journey and not a destination, the successful international management leader thereby finds primary excitement and rewards in the process of achieving success, not in the final state of being successful.

A Note from the Authors

For the past two decades, we have been actively involved in working together in various academic and management training venues in each other's home country, as well as in many other countries. In this process, we have often felt too practical to be theoreticians and too abstract to be practitioners. We have been very lucky and privileged to have had opportunities to work between the two, having been involved with, committed to, and closely associated with organizations and their managements, but having also had the opportunity to look at all of this from an outside perspective. We have learned enormously from the challenges that have emerged—from success and from failure. But it is also important that we have had the opportunity to look at all of this from a distance.

We would be happy if this book provides a real challenge for undergraduate and graduate students in international management, as well as giving practitioners outlines and bases from which to view their own work, their organization, and themselves from a perspective outside the daily hustle and bustle of decision-making. Indeed, the book is an outcome of in-house development projects with this objective.

The framework of this book has been developed with an international perspective. Today, very little truly effective managerial leadership is carried out in isolation from influences of the global village within which economic decisions are made. Thus, international management leadership does become the primary competitive advantage that distinguishes one firm from another.

A given firm may thus have enormous competitive advantages in terms of location, government association, resource availability, preferred or protected markets, etc. However, the manner and degree to which these various competitive advantages are acted upon by the firm to achieve its goals and objectives are focused on the actions of the managerial leaders whose duty it is to give primary direction and overall purpose to the organization.

It is our hope that as a textbook, these pages could also communicate to the student something about the practice of management and life in organizations beyond what is needed to pass a course. In developing the concepts of international management leadership, and helping this subject matter come alive, the authors have drawn from their own experiences as practicing managers, as well as many years in academic and management-development settings.

Raimo W. Nurmi
John R. Darling

Chapter 1

From Moses
to the Third Millennium

*I know of no great men except those who have rendered great
services to the human race.*

—Voltaire

THE EMERGENCE OF MANAGEMENT

The first documents on management date from six millennia ago.
Even earlier and as long as there has been a human society, there
has existed an organization or a division of labor horizontally
between different kinds of tasks and vertically between the many
who labored and the few who led. This is not, however, a book on
the history of management (see, e.g., George, 1972). Instead, we
focus on a few glimpses from the past that have influenced our
thinking about international management leadership today.

The Second Book of Moses (called *Exodus*), which is a Holy
Book for Christians and Jews alike, reports an incident when
Moses, upon leading his people from Egypt to Canaan, grew tired
of the grumbling of the people and stopped to listen to the following
words of his father-in-law, Jethro:

> Be thou for the people to God-ward, that thou mayest bring the
> causes unto God: and thou shalt teach them ordinances and
> laws, and shalt shew them the way wherein they must walk,
> and the work that they must do. Moreover thou shalt provide

out of all the people able men, such as fear God, men of truth, hating covetousness; and place such over them, to be rulers of thousands, and rulers of hundreds, rulers of fifties, and rulers of tens: And let them judge the people at all seasons: and it shall be that, every great matter they shall bring unto thee, but, every small matter they shall judge: so shall it be easier for thyself, and they shall bear the burden with thee. (KJV: Exodus 18; 19-22)

Moses accepted this advice of his consult, Jethro, and implemented the line organization and separated what is today called strategy from what is today called operations and shared the burden or—as it would be said today—delegated tasks to his subordinates, who were to report to Moses in line with *management by exceptions* in present-day management jargon (see Figure 1.1).

Another glimpse dates from 500 B.C. from a text by Lao Tzu:

"A manager is best, when people barely know that he exists. Not so good, when people obey and acclaim him. Worse, when they despise him. Fail to honor people, and they fail to honor you. But of a good manager, who talks little, when his work is done, his aim fulfilled, they will all say: "We did this ourselves." (p. 7)

The Hellenic culture is a foundation of Western Civilization. Many Greek philosophers presented views about organizing and good leadership. But more influential were the ideas that became the essence of Western thinking and Western philosophy. They have influenced our way of seeing organizations and management in a way that even today makes the American and European organizations different from Far Eastern, Islamic, and Black African organizations.

The tradition of Greek analytic thinking remains a fundamental principle contributing to the division of organizations into departments, functions, units, and levels; whereas, other cultures emphasize the unity, the totality, the collectivity, the kinship roles, or the social relations of organizations.

The theory of teleological thinking, developed in the Hellenic period, lay a foundation for goal orientation, which is an essential ingredient in present-day international management leadership

FIGURE 1.1. The Vision of Moses

manifests itself in *management by objectives*, in budgeting, in strategic thinking, and in many other goal-oriented activities.

In the Hellenic city-states, vertical and horizontal division of labor appeared. The free men and the masters of economy, i.e., the leaders, specialized on thinking and politics, delegating all execution to their subordinates—wives, children, and slaves (Figure 1.2). The greatest philosophers of the time created philosophical rationale and justification for this kind of an organization (see, Wagner, 1995, and Cummings, 1995). The idea of separating management from operations is an ancient one, but it was the philosophers of the antique that formulated it in a way that later spread among the many other ideas from this period and were adopted, e.g., by the Christian organizations when they began to take shape. The vertical division of labor between management and operations has remained a key issue of management thinking in the twentieth century.

It is always debatable to date the origin of a discipline or a science. It naturally depends on the varying meanings of the terms *discipline, science,* and *scientific.* Having said that, there are good grounds to argue that it was the philosophers of the antique who were the very first to research management and organization in a way that could be called scientific.

In the Hellinic period, two types of institutions developed that still exist with us and have molded our way of thinking about

Figure 1.2. Aristotle's Organization

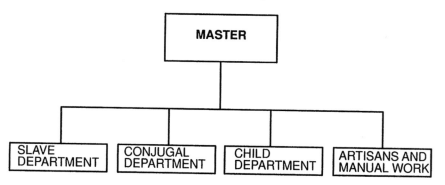

Adapted from Nurmi (1984).

management and organization in a most profound and persistent way, viz, the Church and the Army. Even though their "business ideas" are so different, their managerial and organizational thinking is in many respects strikingly similar. It is true, too, that at times they have found themselves in a close "strategic alliance."

The Catholic Church can be seen as the first truly multinational corporation (MNC). Its sovereign position over peoples and nations was unsurpassed in its heyday. Early in the Middle Ages, the Catholic Church and the armies realized and utilized "the economies of scale." Their widening geographical areas and "market shares" diminished their "unit costs" respectively. The hierarchical difference between the strategic and operative layers was most clear-cut: The top management was raised above all reproach and criticism to infallibility and to represent God—and if the latter did not suffice—the arms on earth.

The Catholic Church and the armies of the Middle Ages founded efficient line and regional organizations, in which the subordinates reported about their obedience to the strategy in the areas of which they were in charge. Standardization of operations and policies was increased, especially in the Church. The use of staff departments increased and stabilized both in the Church and in armies. The horizontal division of labor and specialization grew into an unforeseen level of structuring in the contemporary Church and army.

The influence of the Church, in particular, and that of the armies as well must have been enormous on the organizational thinking of the common people. They taught the people to fear the Lord. The effectiveness of their operations was—considering the contemporary infrastructure—without exaggeration, tremendous. Until this day, no organization has gained a market share as big as that of the Catholic Church at its peak of power. See Figure 1.3 for an illustration of an accountant from the Tudor period. Bookkeeping as a mangerial technique was invented in this era.

Each era has its unique character. Each institution has its own systemic qualities. And each organization has its own gestalt, configuration, field of power, quantum state, integrated circle, process, interactive network. Therefore, too direct a comparison between organizations of centuries ago and present ones must be cautioned. Nonetheless, it is safe to conclude that especially the Church, and in

FIGURE 1.3. An Accountant from the Tudor Period

some realms the armies as well, drilled and exercised people to adopt the kind of views about organizations—e.g., the authority of management—upon which the later industrial organizations found it easy to base their operations.

THE CENTURY OF MANAGEMENT

The early years of this century saw breakthroughs in thinking that were conducive to what we now regard as the beginning of modern management and organization theory. This is due to at least three interdependent background factors. First, industrialization brought with it large companies that created new kinds of organizational problems and solutions, and this created a need for a new kind of organizational thinking. Second, great scientific achievements in new areas consequently increased the demand for their application to organization and management. Third, the values of people and the man in the street in newly grown industrial towns and cities went through a transition so that people began to ask not only for rewards in heaven but also for material well-being on earth as well. All this meant that a new way of thinking about organizations was needed.

It was about this time that the term *management* became of established usage in its present respected meaning. Its root (Italian *maneggiare*) meant horse training in the sixteenth century, and as late as the early eighteenth century, it meant trickery and deceitful contrivance (*Oxford English Dictionary*). The Latin word *manus* means hand, and the hand of the master was, no doubt, early in the history of management, an important source of authority.

Frederick Winslow Taylor is generally recognized to be the founding father of scientific management. His publications in 1903, 1911, and 1912 and his extensive practice of industrial work studies applied thinking and methods derived from science to the study of supervising and organizing. Later, Max Weber introduced the concept of bureaucracy, and it has had a similar influence on administrative organizations. The most mechanistic parts of Taylor's and Weber's ideas became prevalent in the organization literature of the nineteenth century, and the two became, not knowingly, and most probably not willingly, the great theoreticians of mechanistic organizational thinking.

The ideal organizations and the ideal types of mechanical organizations correspond to a well-lubricated machine or machinery. Theoretically, everything and everyone has its proper and determined place in this ideal, but in reality there is not a place for everything nor everyone. The parts of the organization—including people—are seen as disposable elements so that an efficient organization is independent and invulnerable to human weakness and errors. The machine like horizontal and vertical division of labor ascertains the firmness, stability, reliability, and efficiency of the organization. Managers manage; workers work; manufacturing departments specialize in manufacturing, sales departments in selling—and let them not get mixed. A civil servant should stick to the knitting and be careful not to exceed his or her authority. As a part of the machinery, each and every one can grind material effectiveness for his or her organization and receive material compensation as a reward.

Mechanical organization thinking has been criticized, revised, moderated, and recriticized. It has been attacked by human relations, human resource management, systems theory, contingency theory, and a number of other schools of thinking. Organization development, industrial democracy, quality circles, and personnel administration, among others, have been exercised in mechanical organization to make them work in a smoother fashion. Nonetheless, core characteristics of mechanical thinking are easy to discern in today's industry, commerce, and administration. Even the critics have had to admit their unforeseen effectiveness in their most appropriate areas.

World War II upset the entire world and its thinking, and it could not help stirring up management as well. During the war, and even after it, mobilizing, maintaining, and increasing production required an enormous effort, and all this could be achieved only by means of rationalization endeavors. In the special fortieth anniversary issue of *International Management*, August 1986, the development of management methods is illustrated as a coil, where management based on techniques opens up little by little to management based on people (see Figure 1.4). The first two postwar decades witnessed

FIGURE 1.4. Milestones in Management

1946
The word "automation" is coined by Del S. Harder of Ford Motor Co.

International Management Institute is founded in Geneva.

1947
Value Analysis emerges as a management tool at General Electric Co.

1948
Creation of the Organization for European Economic Cooperation, forerunner of the OECD.

Kurt Lewin starts experimental work on group dynamics, leading eventually to sensitivity training.

1958
Foundation of INSEAD management school in Fontainebleau, France. Harold Geneen takes over ITT.

1959
IBM introduces its transistor-based 1401 data-processing system, ushering in the era of second-generation computers.

Late 1950s
Cost-effectiveness analysis blossoms at Rand Corp.

1960
Douglas McGregor expounds his notions of Theory X and Theory Y management in the book *The Human Side of Enterprise*.

Early 1960s
Quality circles make their debut in Japan.

Technological forecasting comes of age with the Delphi technique developed by Rand.

1962
Robert R. Blake and Jane S. Moulton describe their Managerial Grid, which is to attain wide use.

1963
Alfred P. Sloan published *My Years at General Motors*.

Jimmy Ling and Charles Bluhdorn pioneer the age of conglomerates.

General Electric concocts matrix management.

1965-1966
Boston Consulting Group posits the Experience Curve.

1972
The Club of Rome publishes *Limits to Growth*.

The European snake is created to limit currency fluctuations.

1973
First "oil shock" alters the world's economic map.

Harvard sets up a European business program in Switzerland.

Mid-1970s
Sovereign lending becomes big business.

1976
Rambouillet, France is the site of the first economic summit of Western industrial powers.

Late 1970s
"Management by walking around" evolves at Hewlett-Packard.

Early 1970s
Volvo and Saab create "assembly teams" for car production.

Codetermination (trade union representation on boards) catches on in Germany.

Multinationals come under fire for challenging national sovereignty.

Mid-1980s
Merger and acquisition activity explodes in U.S. and spreads to Europe.

1983
In Search of Excellence, by Peters and Waterman, is published.

Harvard terminates its European business program.

FIGURE 1.4 (continued)

1950
The term "office automation" first appears in management literature.

1952
John Diebold publishes *Automation and the Advent of the Automated Factory.*

A. F. Osborne invents the term "brainstorming" in his book *Applied Imagination.*

1954
General Motors installs the first modern industrial robot.

Peter Drucker coins the term "Management by objectives."

General Electric hatches the precursor of Materials Resource Planning, which will start flourishing in the late 1960s.

1955
Texas Instruments establishes the first data-processing center.

1967
Messerschmitt-Bölkow-Blohm introduces flexitime.

Late 1960s
Rapid growth of venture capital companies begins.

1968
The Boston Consulting Group gives birth to stars, dogs, cash cows, and problem children in its widely adopted Portfolio Management matrix.

1969
Einar Thorsrud co-authors *Form and Content in Industrial Democracy.*

Robert Townsend's irreverant *Up the Organization* becomes a best-seller.

1970
General Electric becomes the first major user of Strategic Business Units, as outlined by a McKinsey study.

Mid-1950s
Long-range planning comes into widespread use.

1956
European business school IMEDE is formed in Lausanne.

William H. Whyte's *The Organization Man* is published.

1980
Women hold 3 million of the 11 million management and administrative jobs in the United States.

The One-Minute Manager extols instant management.

Early 1980s
Rescheduling of sovereign debt begins.

Hayes and Abernathy challenge management by numbers in milestone *Harvard Business Review* article.

Harold Green leaves ITT-chairmanship.

1982
The term "intrapreneur" is coined by Norman McCrae writing in *The Economist.*

1971
Richard Nixon terminates the modified gold standard and currencies are floated.

Peter Pyhrr introduces Zero-Based Budgeting.

Treaty of Rome signed, creating the European Economic Community.

1957
C. Northcote Parkinson publishes *Parkinson's Law.*

DuPont adopts critical-path method to improve planning, scheduling, and coordination of new plant construction.

Source: Based on *International Management*, Special 40th Anniversary Issue. August 1986.

automation, value analysis, ideation techniques, management by objectives, automatic data processing, long-range planning, critical path method, and cost-benefit analysis among other techniques. All of these techniques are still with us, although in an adapted, often simplified form, sometimes as a routine.

Douglas McGregor's book *The Human Side of Enterprise* (1960) is a good example of the promoter of people as success factors in business, which is currently in vogue. This capital idea led to many different outcomes and applications such as humanistic management, quality circles, experiments on industrial democracy, organization development, personnel administration, and human resource management, to name just a few. The most influential promoters of a people-oriented management style in the 1980s were very likely Peters and Waterman, whose best-seller in 1983, based on a survey of successful companies, highlighted people and the soft side of management as the more effective approach in business.

This change in emphasis has had solid reasons behind it. In Western countries, management methods and physical resources have been developed extensively, whereas people, their management, and their work are felt to be a much more unpredictable, but a potent and underutilized factor of production and a cornerstone of success. Secondly, the relative importance of services has grown in the developed economies, and within services, its knowledge-intensive sector in particular, (see Nurmi et al., 1992). This sector is based on human know-how and know-why while traditional industries have grown more capital-intensive due to automation. People have changed, too. There are less and less obedient followers and more and more assertive citizens to whom work is not just a necessary toil, but a challenging part of life itself. The cry for meaningful work is more vocal than ever.

There is no doubt that the success story of Japan has made Western businesspeople rethink many of their assumptions on management (see, e.g., Ohmae, 1982). Japanese companies have astonished and, in their competitiveness, frightened many Western managers. Their business excellence seems to have established a unique managerial culture in a country where people are practically the one and only resource. This all is founded on a remarkably strong national identity and culture, which has had their counterparts in a strong organizational identity and organizational culture of the Japanese corporations. This is reflected in what for a Westerner was an unbelievable commitment, diligence, and devotion of the personnel to their companies on the one hand, and, the nearly all-pervasive care that the companies took for their personnel almost from birth to death on the other. The Japanese have been skillful copycats of Western innovations. In fact, they have often made them work better than the innovators were able to do. In selecting American managerial innovations, the Japanese have been geniuses in adopting ideas and modifying them to fit their particular national and organizational cultures. Quality circles and total quality management are prime examples of this kind of ingenuity. However, when Westerners have tried to adopt Japanese management methods, they have not been as successful (see Becker, 1993 and Harari, 1993 for a debate of the concept). All of this has indicated that culture is a much more potent factor in inhibiting or facilitating the transfer and utilization of social inventions than we had formerly realized.

It is mostly due to the business success of the Japanese that culture has become among the most popular topics in recent management literature and management education (Deal and Kennedy, 1982; Smircich, 1983; Schein, 1985; Gahmberg, 1986; Hampden-Turner, 1991). This discussion has shown that corporate culture—such as it reflects itself in beliefs, values, and ways of conduct—affects more than management methods and the skill in their use. Every company has a conscious or an unconscious culture, an internal microculture, which works as a mastermind in the ways of behaving, working, and managing. Its impact is seen in the bottom line, but the transmission is complex and difficult to manage. When a company has done poor for a long time, the turnaround strategy often starts by replacing the top executive, because a leader is in a better position to transform the culture (see, e.g., Byrne, 1993).

Corporate culture manifests itself in management culture. The two cannot be in conflict for long. The success of a company is not based on knowledge, reason, and rational behavior only, but also on beliefs, identities, and commitments. Managers need to sense these—even though they are not manageable in a streamlined fashion. On the other hand, managers do influence organization culture by way of what they do and do not say, by way of what they do and do not do, and particularly when what they say and what they do are in conflict.

Many corporate crises can be interpreted as crises of corporate culture. The cooperative movement in Scandinavia is a case in point. It had a strong cultural, even ideological basis, which lost momentum as seen in decreasing market shares and profitability. The crises in banks, most notoriously in Scandinavian savings banks, was caused by their rejecting in the 1980s their long-established culture based on saving.

Small companies may exhibit a peculiarly strong culture, even if the word *culture* does not belong in the vocabulary of the company. In a small company, the culture is often based on the idea upon which the company was established, and it may be visibly linked to the omnipresent owner-manager-entrepreneur. This very strength of the culture may, however, be a reason for a growth crisis when the company grows beyond the limits of its owner.

Big business extends itself in different countries and different continents—even globally—and is organized as multinational or transnational corporations. These companies are extraordinarily diversified in their products. The various units often have little in common, and it is impossible to govern them in any uniform way. Indeed, the only thing that the units may possibly share is a set of shared values, i.e., a corporate culture. This is why many multinational companies make their core values visible in symbols and artifacts, in logos and slogans, even in uniform conduct and costume, and in meetings that perhaps have more symbolic than business value.

Development is a process of dealing with conflicting forces. It is a dialogue of forces pushing for changes and forces resisting them; it is a battlefield of forces that drive toward different directions. There are strong forces for the human side of management that gained momentum from the 1960s on. But it would be most hypocritical to assert that work and management have been humanized only recently. Indeed, the 1990s have witnessed a reaction, and managers have had to make difficult, tough, even repulsive decisions.

The economies in many countries have slowed down and even declined. Adapting to a depression is a painful process. Mistakes from the booming 1980s—in the financial sector, neglect of productivity, etc.—have urged many companies to replace managers with new people whose credibility is not stained with past mistakes. International interdependence creates sudden crises that spread from the epicenter literally overnight, such as in the finance markets. Formation of the European Union has opened up markets, broken down protectionistic barriers, intensified competition, and inevitably compelled national companies to radical transformations.

It has remained almost unnoticed that management skill will be the competitive advantage to a much greater extent than it ever was in national markets, where the number of suppliers remain limited and competition can be avoided by mutual agreements of the suppliers. The opening up of the Eastern European region in all its unpredictability has required abrupt structural changes in countries and companies that had considerable markets in former communist countries (see Uksvärav, 1991). These companies have to their regret noticed that by concentrating on the Eastern markets, they lost their competitiveness in the West—not only competitiveness of products, prices, design, and quality, but basically competitiveness in management.

These transformations have already caused severe crises in many companies. There is no easy way out of them. Undecisiveness is the worst strategy. Axing costs; reshuffling companies; cutting personnel; closing departments, plants, and companies; reorganizing debts—all these and other crisis measures galore exist (see Tomasko, 1987). Acquisitions and takeovers are often decided beyond the bounds of managers, but managers must carry out the consequences in their office as well as in person. These kinds of unpleasant transformations have tried all people from managerial echelons down to the rank and file. Consequences include an increased and a new kind of unemployment, changes in and impairment of the quality of work, a change of emphasis from developing to cutting, from the future outlook to a survival game in the short run.

It is difficult, but important, to have a future outlook, especially in the middle of crises. We bear the risk of being so troubled in solving daily problems that we lose sight of what lurks around the corner. Time will solve some of the problems with which we busy ourselves. There are more persevering ones, no doubt, and the way we work on them today will make or break the future. The key is to see into the future and the opportunities it provides us. Many of the threats of today are opportunities of tomorrow for those who can look beyond the present to what lies ahead on the horizon.

THEORIES OF MANAGEMENT

The practice of management has changed when businesses and business environments have changed. The twentieth century has also seen the birth of management studies as a discipline. Some call it a science. Management studies do not develop in a vacuum; they reflect what is going on in management practice.

Management studies is a subject of many orientations. For this reason, Koontz (1961, 1980) calls it a jungle. These are empiricists who try to observe management practices as they are exercised; there are theorists who attempt to describe management by abstracting its essential qualities; there are normative thinkers who describe what management should do; there are practicianers who work toward the development of better management practices. These are just a few of an endless list of orientations. Besides, we have begun to be aware that management and management studies are culturally bound and that they are exercised in different parts of the world in varying forms despite the fact that the Western and predominantly American view is hegemonic in management textbooks.

This is not a treatise on management studies nor management theories. Nonetheless, a brief account of the most influential management theories of our century is appropriate since they have had a considerable influence on management practices, and traces of them are visible in contemporary management techniques. Any attempt to develop management practice depends upon what is considered the essence of management. "What is the essence of management?" is a proper question for management theory to answer. Different theories give different answers to this question. Additionally, a theory should describe relationships between the essential parts of management.

In everyday speech, theory is often considered alien or even opposed to practice. Nothing could be more misleading. A theory shows what is essential in the complex world of reality and outlines relationships of the essential elements. A theory is an abstraction of reality, but a valid theory cannot be in conflict with reality (see Figure 1.5). A theory that discerns essentials from nonessentials and even relates them with each other could be a most practical conceptual orientation in the jungle of practice for any manager.

True enough, it is not quite as simple as that. Admittedly, constructing useful theories is not easy. Available management theories are far from exact; they are not valid under different circumstances nor are they able to predict outcomes of different management actions. At best, they are orientation maps that relate different vistas to each other. This is not a poor achievement, though, and in the mind of an experienced manager, this kind of an orientation map is quite useful. Management theories do not operate on paper, but only in the minds of their users and appliers. No theory can replace a thinking and responsi-

FIGURE 1.5. The Relationship of Theory and Reality

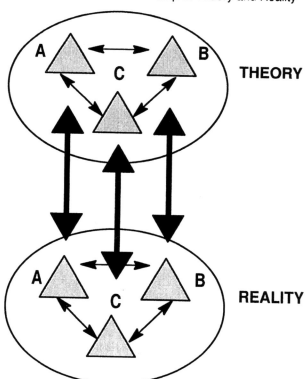

ble manager, but it sure helps if one can work on the essentials and see how working on one affects the others.

As a matter of fact, all of us have a theory of practice. We all see some points as more essential than the rest, and we assume some kind of a relation between them. Our theory of reality is more or less conscious for us, and it affects the way we act. In this sense, theory and practice are always connected in the world of management. In the following, the most influential theories of the twentieth century are briefly introduced by simplifying the original thoughts. They are presented in the approximate order of their publication.

Scientific Management

Scientific management is considered the first "modern" theory of management. Taylor is its best-known proponent to such a degree that the work-study movement is called Taylorism. Work study is a method of analyzing and measuring industrial work in its smallest units and movements, and it was initiated to increase productivity in factories. World War I and the need to boost wartime production when resources grew limited, boosted Taylorism as well. In the United States, mass production of cars after the war applied its methodology. Fordism is another label attached to the movement. In the former Soviet Union, Taylorism was adopted quite early, and it was named after Alexei G. Stakhanov, the model worker for a communist society who had been recognized for exceeding prodution norms.

Apart from being a methodology to study and intensify work, scientific management launched ideas of division of labor that can be seen as steps toward a theory of management and organization. The most influential of the ideas has been the clear-cut demarcation between management (or supervision) and the operative work. Managerial work is to plan and control and to delegate doing to the worker (Figure 1.6). It was this demarcation of doing from planning and control for which Taylor was later criticized by others.

Administrative School

The administrative school was developed in Europe, and the Frenchman Fayol published his thesis during the emergence of

FIGURE 1.6. Tayloristic Vertical Division of Labor

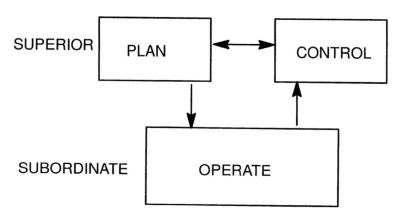

Taylorism in the United States. The ideas became generally known only in the 1920s. Fayol defined management as the loop and trinity of planning, operating, and control (Figure 1.7). This loop is called management process, and its parts developed into functions of management. Later, other functions of management were added, such as staffing, organizing, decision making, etc. This idea of management process is one of the most permanent in the management literature. It manifests itself in management practices, e.g., management by objectives includes this idea in its core. Job enrichment programs have introduced the trinity of planning, operating, and control down to the shop floor in companies like Texas Instruments, Olivetti, IBM, Volvo, and Saab, as well as in many construction and glass-making factories.

Bureaucracy

Bureaucracy as a school of management includes standing procedures, rules, policies, and regulations as central management methods. Max Weber's (1978) voluminous production includes a well-known and much-quoted account on bureaucracy, and his ideas greatly influenced public administration. Despite vehement criticism leveled against bureaucracy—it is often used as a metaphor for

FIGURE 1.7. The Trinity of Planning, Operating, and Control

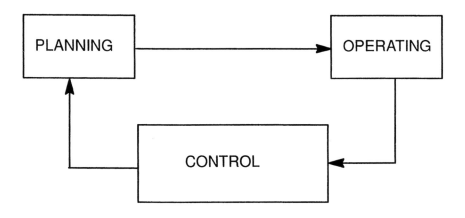

ineffectiveness—it has left easily discernable traces in our manage-ment thinking as well. Rules and standing procedures are consid-ered a necessity, albeit definitely not the most important ingredients in management. Bureaucracy keeps things going, but it encourages neither change nor excellent performance. In a bureaucracy, follow-ing the rules is more important than results. This view is too com-mon in parts of public administration, but all corporations are not free from it either. Bureaucracy has a tendency to live and expand in excess; hence, management needs to watch it and, at times, reshuffle and cut it.

All these theoretical schools are characterized by impersonality. Management, or administration, is an almost automatic, impersonal, and logical function. As a reaction, a number of theories emerged that emphasized the human side of management.

Human Relations/Resources

Human relations as a movement claimed that the most important task for a manager is to promote human relations in the company. This would increase the satisfaction of people, and the satisfied people, in turn, would perform well and improve the performance of the company. As this formulation was proved too naive (e.g., Staw and Barsade, 1993), it was reconceptualized as human resources. According to this view, the most important task of a manager is to mobilize and utilize human resources to serve company objectives. As this view turned out to be biased as well, a number of leadership theories appeared; in these, concern for people is one factor as is concern for production (e.g., Likert, 1961; Blake and Mouton, 1964; 3D by Reddin, 1970). In this thinking, it is the task of management to integrate the two dimensions (see Figure 1.8).

Great Man Theory

The great man theory of leadership lives probably more in biographies (Sloan, 1972; Iacocca, 1984), management magazines (e.g., Taylor, 1993), and popular views than in critical studies of management. According to this, great managers are great men and women with unique leadership qualities that emerge particularly on unique occa-

FIGURE 1.8. Managerial Grid

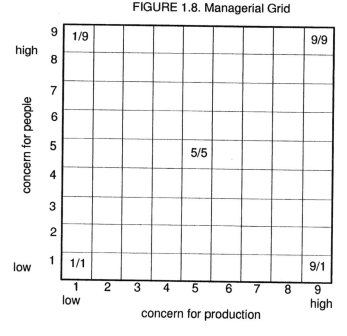

Source: Blake and Mouton (1971).

sions (Roddick, 1991). Empirical studies have tried to discern correlations of personal traits with leadership effectiveness and efficiency. The results have been meager and conflicting. Good leaders may be equipped with a myriad of different traits (see Lipshitz and Nevo, 1992). Some traits may show a curvilinear relationship. For example, a manager needs to have a minimum level of intelligence, but geniuses are not the best communicators with the average majority. More important than leadership traits are the interaction of the leaders and the resources of the group (see Magnusen, 1995).

Systems Theory

Systems theory was a promising newcomer in the management field a couple of decades ago. According to a classic definition, "a system is a set of parts coordinated to accomplish a set of goals" (Churchman, 1977). This approach describes management as a system of related elements and by so doing attempts to capture the comprehensiveness of the phenomenon. It had a promise to integrate the field and to show the other theories—valid in their proper but limited area—their place as parts of the whole system. Theory of control was developed by this approach. The Scandinavian School (Rhenman, 1973) has been active academically and also in consulting under the auspices of the Scandinavian Institute of Administrative Research. In corporate planning and in long-range planning, systems had their day. Management by objectives had systems applications. Mathematical models were elaborated and sophisticated. In the former Soviet Union, cybernetic models were a socialist counterpart of systems thinking. The turbulences, unpredictability of changes, downright messes, and muddles of the early 1990s seemed for a while, at least, to make systems thinking obsolete. But systems thinking is still alive in some areas of management and particularly in information systems. Besides, the history of management thinking shows that what has been considered obsolete after a few decades from its conception may reappear revised, refurbished, refreshed, and new after another decade or two.

Contingency Theory

During the 1970s, contingency theory or situational theory made the mainstream of theoretical thinking in management and organization literature. It argues that there are no general management principles at all. Instead, it is the fit between the management (and organization) and its situational factors that determines effectiveness. Woodward (1965) and Pfeffer and Salancik (1978) serve as two dissimilar examples of this very general notion. Situational factors, in turn, are outside the organization. Markets and technology are two important parts of the environment, and management must be compatible with these situational factors in order to succeed. Situational flexibility, strategic vision, and the ability to endure transformations are of prime importance in this thinking. This is, of course, a view that is in accordance with times of abrupt change. The problem that a manager may feel using contingency theory is that it leaves him* in an everything-depends-on-everything enigma, without necessary clues of what is essential, how things are related, how to analyze the multitude of situations, and how to orient in the jungle. Practice in management does show, however, some regularities between situational factors and management. So, in a business downturn and in a survival game, management gets more centralized, authoritarian, even dictatorial, and business is conducted at the expense of the human side of it. In better times, developing and investing in tangibles and intangibles grow in importance. As obvious as this is, it shows that if situations could be typologized, contingency theory could work as a useful compass in the complicated situational map of management.

In the 1980s, a gamut of theories emerged, probably too many for us to see which of them will have a permanent influence and which of them were merely fads. Role theories have a long history, but they clearly had a revival, e.g., in Mintzberg and Adizes (1979). This will be scrutinized in the next chapter.

Managerialism

Managerialism, though deriving from Peter Drucker's writings back in the 1950s, got a new impetus in its criticism and opposition

---

*Until recently, management has been viewed as predominantly a male function. Hence, the male "he" is appropriate in the history of management. By the middle of the twentieth century, women were entering managerial positions and, undoubtly, this trend will continue and affect management. However, it would be clumsy to use the phrase "he or she" every time the third person is used. For this reason, "he" and "she" are interchangably used in this book generically.

to contingency theory. In a way, the two are complementary. Managerial margin is a crucial concept in this new formulation. There are managerial arenas in which situational factors are so stringent as to leave little margin for management to influence. During a depression, markets may leave little for the management to maneuver in the short run at least. But there are other arenas in which management is a decisive factor. Strategic management is generally considered this kind of an arena. Now, new revival in managerialism asks for an assessment of situational factors so that management could use the margin optimally seizing opportunities without allocating time and energy where they would not pay off. Indeed, this principle was recognized by St. Francis of Assisi from the thirteenth century:

> Lord,
> Give me the power to change what I can change.
> Give me the patience to stand what I cannot change.
> Give me the wisdom to see the difference between the two.

Managerialism and situationalism are engaged in an everlasting dialogue in management thinking. It can be asserted that managerialism is the more pragmatic of the two. Extreme situationalism would make defeatism a virtue. Managerialism, instead, gives hope that man and his intentions can change the world. Managerialism is a pragmatic assumption in the practice and study of management. There is empirical research evidence that managers do matter (e.g., Miller, Kets de Vriese, and Toulouse, 1982; Gupta and Govindarajan, 1984). This is not a revival of the great man theory, though. Rather, the studies refer to strategic choice as the key influence of managers. There are environmental constraints, but within them, the strategic choice of management has a dynamic role to play (see Stacey, 1995).

In the 1990s, traces from these theoretical developments remain conspicuous, mingled with each other, and continuously reformulated. Management continues to include planning, operating, and control. Rules and regulations have not been omitted either. Concern for people is a growing issue. Managers apply systems. Situational factors remind managers of contingencies and the parameters of their actions. The leading theoretical ideas are very much alive, but a consistent synthesis of them remains so far a dream.

The theorists of the early 1990s seem to have been most interested in strategic management and corporate culture. Management, managers, and leadership are viewed as a kind of agent between the company and the environment; managers have to transform their companies to make them fit with the environment, but managers can also influence the environment for the successful fit by stretching the resources of their organization (see Hamel and Prahalad, 1993). The issue can be formulated in terms of markets (environmental factor) and hierarchies (organizational factor) as control mechanisms (McGuinness, 1991). Schein (1985) would add cultures and Ouchi (1980) clans; Powell (1990) would argue for networks as the best way to understand the management of modern organizations. These ongoing debates are most vivid and appear in management practices. They are dealt with and fused in the chapters that follow.

REVIEW QUESTIONS

1. What characteristics of mechanical organizations can you indentify in present-day companies?

2. Which developments from postwar history of management are most visible in present-day management?

3. Which developments from the 1990s would you add to the cavalcade of postwar management thinking?

4. Which management theories are most influential today?

5. What does contingency theory imply?

LEARNING EXERCISES

Analyze your job and identify the five points in it that are the most important for task accomplishment.

Place these five points in the five circles below. Describe the relations of the points by arrows between the circles.

FIGURE 1.9. Job analysis model

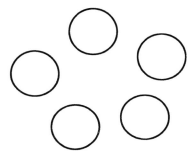

Now you have actually constructed a kind of a theory of your job. Give it a name and name the figure accordingly. What did you learn about the "theory"?

How does your theory relate itself to other ideas and thoughts in the chapter?

Chapter 2

The Environment of Management

A major step toward success is taken when you refuse to be a captive of the environment in which you find yourself.

—Mark Caine

THE EMERGENCE OF THE THIRD MILLENNIUM

The trend that affects all that we do in management is a new impetus for internationalization. Even if we remain in our native country, we cannot avoid the world coming to us. To companies and people alike, this implies an active search of and entrance into world markets. At the same time, the structure of the world economy goes through transitions that affect all national economies (see e.g., Toffler, 1990). Additionally, the integration of Western Europe and the disintegration of Eastern Europe will provide us with many surprises. Paradigms of science have been challenged. The values of man are changing, and the values of industrial society are disintegrating in a process whose outcome nobody can predict.

It was these three transitions—one in the structure of economy, another in the escalation of science, and the third in values of man— that gave birth to management and organization thinking early in the twentieth century. The contemporary challenge in all of them must challenge our thinking about organizations and their management accordingly (Figure 2.1).

As a new millennium looms on the horizon, the human curiosity to peek into the future gets irresistible. Many of the future factors are already among us, though it is hard for us to distinguish the essential from the less essential. Again and again in the history of humankind,

FIGURE 2.1. The Parallel Levels of Transition at the Change of the Millennium

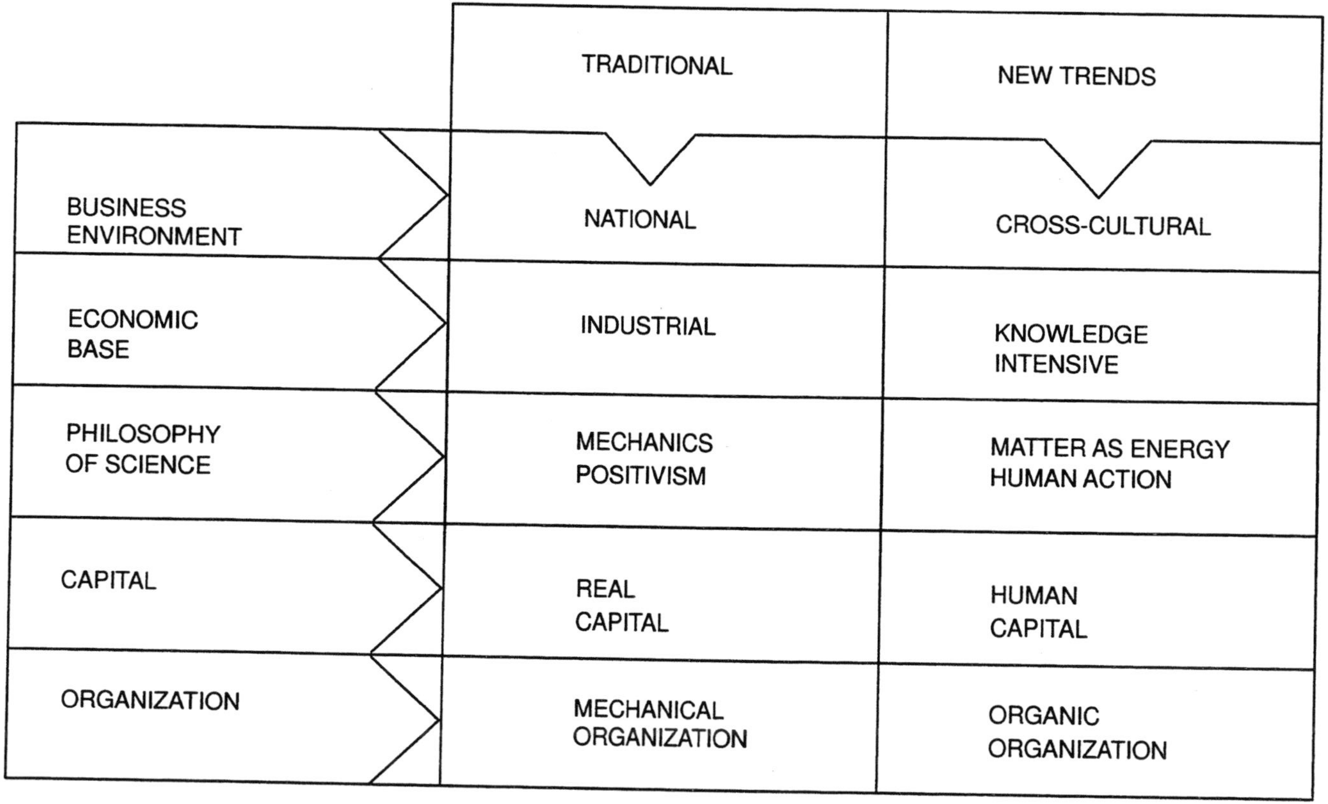

	TRADITIONAL	NEW TRENDS
BUSINESS ENVIRONMENT	NATIONAL	CROSS-CULTURAL
ECONOMIC BASE	INDUSTRIAL	KNOWLEDGE INTENSIVE
PHILOSOPHY OF SCIENCE	MECHANICS POSITIVISM	MATTER AS ENERGY HUMAN ACTION
CAPITAL	REAL CAPITAL	HUMAN CAPITAL
ORGANIZATION	MECHANICAL ORGANIZATION	ORGANIC ORGANIZATION

the tides of events have witnessed humans' inability to foresee what is to come. Indeed, the turbulences in the world exemplified in economics and politics at the change of the last decade of our millennium stand as primary examples of this. Managers, in particular, are by the very nature of their job so busy in solving present predicaments that it is hard for them to detach themselves sufficiently from this day and vision the future.

Management manages the future instead of predicting it. We all affect the future today by what we do—some, admittedly, are nearer to the corridors of power than others. Through hindsight, we can realize that the seeds of the changes we have undergone have been in the past, even though the contemporaries had trouble seeing them. All possible futures are not as possible. A manager needs imagination to be able to influence the future. But he also must see the margin in which he can operate. Futuristic literature can challenge the imagination, but it can also give clues about probabilities of different futures. It does not give valid enough predictions for managerial use, but it triggers a manager's own thinking. This is, in fact, true of all management literature and learning.

Figure 2.2 illustrates one future vision, viz. the *Megatrends 2000* of Naisbitt and Aburdene. It is based on an optimistic interpretation of a vast amount of material. It has been among the most influential triggers of managerial thinking. However, some of its items are already

FIGURE 2.2. A Future Outlook

- The Booming Global Economy of the 1990s
- A Renaissance in the Arts
- The Emergence of Free-Market Socialism
- Global Lifestyles and Cultural Nationalism
- The Privatization of the Welfare State
- The Rise of the Pacific Rim
- The Decade of Women in Leadership
- The Age of Biology
- The Religious Revival of the New Millennium
- The Triumph of the Individual

Source: Adapted from Naisbitt and Aburdene (1990).

dated. These kinds of lists are not useless, even if they do not prove to be completely correct. Their point is to pay attention to crucial signals to be acted upon. This very acting can turn the tide of events. For this purpose, *Megatrends 2000* makes quite useful reading.

Figures 2.3 and 2.4 are based on another future outlook—the one collected by Coates and Jarratt (1989), who interviewed 17 leading futurologists for the purpose. In their study, they acknowledge uncertainties. Their outlook is not a prediction either, but an informed and educated vision. So far, the visions collected with this methodology have proved more conservative than bold.

FROM NATIONAL
TO CROSS-CULTURAL MANAGEMENT

In Western Europe, the national states have turned out to be too small for corporations to operate within. When their home markets have become saturated, they have started to internationalize. Western European integration is accelerating the process. The opening of East-

FIGURE 2.3. What Futurists Believe

- Complexity
- Governments and Institutions Unable to Cope with Complexity
- The Dominance of Science and Technology
    — Telematics
    — Biotechnology
    — Materials
- The Importance of Solving the Energy Transition
- Slowdown of World Economic Growth
- Transition with Continuity
- The Avoidance of Nuclear War
- Interdependence of the Globe
- Decline of the United States
- Education Requires Much Improvement
- Demands of the Information Society
- Aging of the Population in Developed Countries

Source: Adapted from Coates and Jarratt (1989).

FIGURE 2.4. Uncertainties Futurists Acknowledge

- The Ability of Societies to Change Without Disasters
- World Population Growth
- Military, Defense, and Disarmament
- Africa
- Values and Attitudes
- The World's Ability to Build a Global Infrastructure
- The Emancipation of Women
- Environmental Problems
- Nations, Nation Groups, Nationalities, and Nationalism
- Unanticipated Effects of Technological Change
- Optimistic vs. Pessimistic Images of the Future

Source: Adapted from Coates and Jarratt (1989).

ern Europe is also creating new business opportunities for Eastern and Western companies. American companies have likewise confronted limitations in their huge home-markets, and European and especially Japanese companies have come to compete with and even beat American companies in the domestic market. Japan has been the most advanced in this process, but the whole Pacific Rim has followed suit. Oil-producing countries have had increasing influence due to their control of oil reserves. The future of the Third World will either remain as it is or start a new trajectory depending on whether the Third World countries partake in international mutual exchange.

Internationalization means that we have to go to the world and learn to cope with it. The world will also certainly come to us, whether we want it or not. Isolation is not a viable strategy. This development cannot occur without pain, crises, and turmoil (see Adler, 1995; Markides and Stopford, 1995). But it is up to executives, in particular, to make it happen as peacefully as possible. At any rate, economic and information warfare is not as devastating as military warfare. Economic and information competition creates possibilities for development, division of labor, and cooperation on a much higher level than wars have ever done or could ever do.

Internationalization in all is a many-faceted process (see, e.g., Hodgetts and Luthans, 1991). It is here treated only from one particular angle that is significant in international management, that is culture and cross-cultural management. Acquisitions and mergers of companies vary from difficult to incredibly difficult due to cultural collisions, even between companies in the same country (see Fairburn and Geroski, 1989; Larsson, 1990). The difficulties are encountered in the second power, when the acquired or merging company belongs to another national culture. Then the clashes of two organizational cultures (microculture level) and two national cultures (macroculture level) are confronted at the same time. For this reason, joint ventures are a most difficult form of cooperation (see Liuhto's 1991 research material). Joint ventures do have a tremendous potential for synergy: If the strengths of the two can be combined, the performance is raised to the second power as well (see Harris and Moran, 1987).

Culture is a whole, containing elements that are interdependent. A change in one element succeeds or fails depending on how the changed element fits in with the totality of the culture (see Lewin, 1935, for an early account and Earley and Singh, 1995, for a recent review). Time and again, a well-thought and well-resourced change has failed to materialize because it has been in conflict with the core values of a culture. Dramatic examples are abundant in developing countries in attempts to transfer Western technology without giving due notice to the values of the people who are supposed to use the technology. Many wonderful machines and devices have become rusty in deserts and jungles because they have not been congruent with the local culture.

Management is much more culture-bound than hard technology is (see Nurmi and Udo-Aka, 1980; Zaheer, 1995). Management is most intricately interwoven with people and their values, which are dependent on reference groups outside the company and even in the past. For instance, Western ("modern") time-management techniques are impossible to use in cultures where the time concept is strikingly different. Time is not money in many areas in Eastern Europe, Moslem countries, Latin America, and Black Africa. Then, our concepts of budgeting, objectives, planning, or strategic thinking do not directly apply in these cultures. Another business example is that what we regard as corrupt or nepotistic practices are the normal grease for the wheels in many parts of the world.

It is true that technology and management may have had a significant impact on culture as well. Just think of how cars, telecommunication, and microprocessing have influenced our lifestyles. International corporations have succeeded in transferring technology and management know-how. But this kind of influence is a long process, in which the impact of a single manager remains limited. Besides, these transfer processes seldom come true in the intended way, and they are apt to have unintended side effects. Executives are paid to have an impact; hence, it is too easy for them at the outset of their first international assignment to overestimate their chances in an alien culture. Likewise, the difficulties of importing a management practice that works, say in Japan, to another culture are not easily foreseen. At any rate, a company-specific adaptation and digesting are needed. Even then, management practices that are in a vehement conflict with deeper cultural values have little chance to succeed. A major change in a macroculture takes place more often as an outcome of a crisis than as a result of intended management. It is true, though, that the efforts of management may create a deadlock, but what follows is more difficult to control. Think of Reza Shah Pahlevi or Mikhail Gorbachev!

In the following, a brief review of Western, Islamic, Far Eastern, and Black-African core values is presented. Admittedly, the presentation remains superficial, as all the four cultural and geographical areas have a wide spectrum of subcultures within each of them (cf. Nurmi, 1986). Even so, this discussion of different core values provides an indication of the wide variety of values and shows that values are much less universal and objective than most people tend to comprehend due to cultural myopia.

Western Culture

The core value in the Western culture is the relationship of *man to material*. Western culture is the most materialistic of all the cultures on earth. This has resulted in material success, a progressive technology and know-how, an emphasis on work and competence (particularly in the Protestant countries), the linear time-concept, an analytic mode of thinking, measurement of results, and productivity as a focus of human endeavor. These values explain the technological and economic effectiveness of the West. Some cultures use themselves as their model. Many Western people see their values universally valid and objective. Nothing could be more incorrect!

Islamic Culture

In Islam, the core value is the relationship of *man to God*. Religion has shaped the Western culture for thousands of years by many discernable and undiscernible means, too. But today in the West, religion as an institution has much less influence on business behavior and ethics in a modern corporation. For a Muslim, religion comes first, and it provides codes for business conduct and other spheres of life. Being a true Muslim is seen in public conduct, and it is valued more than competence and performance. Due to their oil, many Arab countries have grown in importance in the world economy (and politics). Without realizing the religious core values of the Arabs, there is little chance to understand their conduct—especially in business.

Far Eastern Culture

In the Far East, the core value is the relationship of *man to collectivity*. The economic success of the Far East Tigers (e.g., Japan, South Korea, and Taiwan) has been founded in the willingness of men and women to dedicate themselves for their collectivities. The present-day collectivities are well known in the West; some examples are Canon, Hyundai, and Sony. The core value appears in a collective, time-consuming decision making, the quick implementation of decisions, life-long recruitment of company people instead of specialists rotating between companies, and the long daily, weekly, and yearly working hours. Japanese management remains a mystery to those who do not see how it developed from the core values of the culture.

Black-African Culture

In Black Africa, the core value is the relationship of *man to man*. This concept fosters an emphasis on family, kinship, the primacy of emotions, symbolism, rhythm, and the integrity of man and soul (animism). The time concept is cyclical, and in this concept, time is not at a premium. In recruitment, family, kinship, and tribe are far more important than competence. For a Westerner, this is nepotism; for an African, the Western practice is cold and inhuman. Even "formal" organizations in Black Africa are influenced by kinship ties.

Characterizations of these four cultures are sweeping, even stereotyping generalizations. The tapestry of cultures and core values is much more colorful and shifting. But even with its shortcomings, this brief discussion of macrocultures provides a glimpse of the enormous variety of cultural values that we all are apt to lose sight of in our inherent cultural myopia. Anyone going to work in an alien country should thoroughly learn about its culture. For this purpose, we discuss next the roots and consequences of culture (see Figure 2.5). This discussion provides the reader with a checklist of items that are pertinent in learning about any culture.

Figure 2.5 shows that a culture and its core values are intricately interwoven with an abundance of antecedent factors. Culture's consequences are manifold, and these consequences, in turn, shape the antecedents. The consequences of culture, in turn, shape the antecedent factors. This explains why the change of a culture is such a cumbersome process, as a change in one of its elements interacts with a host of other elements. If an intended change of an element is resisted by the rest of the elements, the change does not succeed, and the unintended results outweigh the intended one. Culture is conservative; it resists change; it maintains the equilibrium of its elements. Figure 2.5 is elaborated in an attempt to illustrate the items in the figure as elements of culture.

Geography is a major determinant of a national culture. So, in continental Europe the geographical proximity of relatively small nations has produced an abundance of cultures. They have much in common, but they also assert their national uniqueness in ways that at times lead to conflicts. As an opposition to the European proximity, Blaney (1966) interprets the history and culture of Australia in terms of the "tyranny of distance," or the geographical distance from Europe as well as between the early Australian settlements.

Weather is another given. Its influence on culture becomes evident to anyone who traverses Europe from the Mediterranean to the North. In the Mediterranean countries, people live and socialize out

FIGURE 2.5. Roots and Consequences of Culture

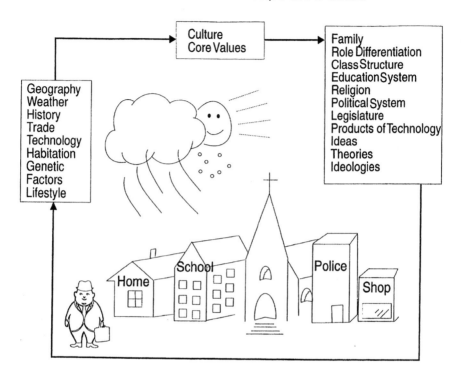

in the open and out of doors. Beyond the Alps, even people grow cooler. Further up in the North, the temperament turns serious and reticent, which reflects the dark, cold winters (see Nurmi, 1990).

History is the father of culture. Culture has a long memory, and history is its collective memory. The values that a country has once cherished are not easily erased from the collective consciousness, even under suppression. This is obvious in the Eastern European disintegration: The countries that experienced a national independence and market economy between the two World Wars have fewer difficulties in their present transition than countries that did not have this experience (see Sagers and Johnson, 1991).

Trading is not an exchange of goods only. It is also an exchange of culture. Business negotiations sometimes fail as the participants fail to recognize different cultural assumptions (see Kapoor, Hansen and Davidson, 1991). Cultures also vary in the relative importance they give to trade. The Arab countries have been in the crossroads of Europe, Asia, and Africa during all documented history, and their tradition and skill in trading can today be observed by anyone visiting a genuine Arab bazaar.

Technology is a prime determinant of all change, including cultural change. Just think of the difference in lifestyle that the car and television have caused. The adoption of modern technology is modified by culture, and the transfer of technology is often moderated by values of people. Birth control is an appropriate example of a technique that is unacceptable in many parts of the world due to religious values.

Habitation has changed in almost all the world from rural to urban, and values have changed accordingly. People in congested cities have a dramatically different lifestyle than people in isolated villages. In some countries, the preference to own a house or a flat leads to a high degree of saving, while in some countries the preference to rent a house leads to another type of economic behavior.

Even though culture is learned and is not transmitted by genes, *genetical predisposition* makes it easier for some people(s) to adopt one set of values rather than another. Little is known about these predispositions, and the concept of "national character" has a dubious history and a sensitive presence. Yet, we know that the amount of inbreeding varies between cultures and subcultures, and it produces corresponding predispositions that have their cultural consequences.

The Western core family, the polygamy in Islamic countries, the subordination of family to the corporation in Japan, and the extended family in the Black Africa are obvious reflections of the respective core values.

Sex roles are perceptible in the roles that women play in a society. In the West, women are relatively emancipated. In the Islamic countries and in the Far East, women are subservient to men, though in very different ways. In Black Africa, women are active in business and they are the working sex in general. Even within Western countries, there are wide differences regarding the role of women in society and business.

The differentiation of *social class* varies enormously between cultures. Sometimes the class distinctions are clearly visible and explicit.

But even in relatively egalitarian cultures, there are class distinctions that are not easily discerned by a foreign eye. "It is impossible for an Englishman to open his mouth without making some other Englishman despise him" (George Bernard Shaw, *Pygmalion*) refers to the connection of class and spoken language in English society. In some areas of the United States, people sharing a particular religion, birth place, or national origin have risen to higher echelons of society than individuals who did not belong to the particular group.

The role of *education* as a social ladder is culture-specific. In Scandinavia, there has been a tendency to standardize education and degrees so that a degree in one school corresponds with the same degree from another school. In many countries, schools and their degrees vary, and schools are ranked as much as the degrees. So in the United States, a graduate from Harvard or Yale may have a better market value than a graduate from a school that does not belong to the Ivy League.

Religion is in the quintessence of culture. It is most conspicuous in Islamic countries. Even in countries where religion is less conspicuous, it is a significant element in the collective memory of a culture. In Protestant countries, the Protestant work ethic has remained longer than has attendance to the Protestant church service. Religions are—as we have seen much to our horror—even now a major legitimation for brutal wars. Religion is an intricately discreet issue, and an international businessman had better avoid it in business negotiations.

Despite the collapse of communism, there is still a gamut of *political* systems. (Besides, Homo Sovieticus, the common thread of the Soviet heritage, is long-enduring in the minds of humans despite the collapse of the system. Nurmi and Üksvärav, 1993, and Üksvärav and Nurmi, 1993). Embargoes are another example of political influence on business. Small countries are often afraid that big countries in their economic and business cooperation create political dependence.

Legislature is far from similar in different parts of the world. Scandinavian countries have relied on legalism; therefore, laws abound, and enacting laws is seen as a solution, whereas the British would agree on a convention. In the United States, extensive federal legislature is seen as a threat to individual freedom, but at the same time, the business law and legal procedures are so complicated that it is always good advice for any foreigner starting a business in the United States to recruit a lawyer first. The European Union is notorious for its directives, but the cultural diversity of Europe is reflected in how different states react to them. In the Mediterranean area, the directives are signed and forgotten, while the British oppose and resist, and in the Nordic countries, they are taken very seriously in the national legislature.

The tangible and intangible *products* of a nation (technology, ideas, theories, ideologies) reflect its culture as well. It would be as difficult to imagine the car being invented in Black Africa as an Islamic revolution occurring in the United States.

This lengthy, yet cursory illustration of roots and consequences of culture and the complex interrelatedness of its elements emphasizes that culture is a given to a newcomer in it. A newcomer had better learn about it instead of attempting to make it work at his will. The items in Figure 2.5 can be seen as a checklist for anyone who intends to go to work in an alien culture. Studying the foreign country item by item and comparing it to one's own culture makes many things easier to understand. Then, a single element that to a foreigner appears to be incomprehensible, quaint, or stupid becomes comprehensible in the context of the whole culture and its interrelated elements. Misunderstanding is never completely unavoidable, but proper preparation helps keep one from enduring unnecessary pains or from hurting local counterparts. This would help the newcomer avoid too severe a culture shock (see Black, Mendenhall, and Oddou, 1991, for a comprehensive treatment of adjustment to a culture).

FROM MECHANICAL TO ORGANIC ORGANIZATIONS

Traditional industries will remain significant and weighty. Their automatization will accelerate along with informatics, which will intrude into interorganizational connections and networks as well (see Suomi, 1990). Human resources on the operational level are needed less and mainly in process control and maintenance tasks. As the operations become increasingly mechanized, the top management's prime concern will be strategic issues, for many industries are entering an intense global competition of survival, death, or fusion. While the operations will become more and more mechanized, the management will be more and more knowledge-intensive. Indeed, the success of internationalization will depend on the management's know-how and know-why. The turning around of industrial giants takes a wide radius, and the mechanization of the organizations makes quick movements more cumbersome. These factors do not make the management of traditional and mature industries easier. Personnel administration, human resource management, and industrial relations remain important, and the monotony of work may lead to new kinds of industrial disturbances. Wages remain important as many people work in monotonous jobs to earn their living.

On a par with traditional mechanical organizations in industry and public administration, organic types of organizations have grown particularly in services and in knowledge-intensive business. Their share in employment and in value-added is considerably bigger than their share in gross domestic product, turnover, or other measures of gross volume. They are grounded on the know-how and know-why of their operative personnel.

The operative person is the subject of action in knowledge-intensive business. The organization of such a business is organic instead of mechanic (see Figure 2.6). The persons must have an intrinsic motivation to work, and entreprenurship, intrapreneurship, and a high level of competence are needed in order to be able to work in an organic organization. Too-close management and organization inhibit the self-determined creativity and spontaneous interaction of people. People perform better by their intrinsic motivation than by administrative fiat. The operative people have access even to strategic information, as they have the direct contact with the product-market mix. Then, the communication from them to the management is more critical than the flow of top-to-down information. Organization grows flat, and the distance between the management and the operations remains short. This facilitates communication, but it also renders managerial control and coordination complex. Self-control, coordination, and communication between the persons concerned must be relied upon.

In case the raw material of a company is information that the company processes into knowledge-intensive products or services, the industrial management and organization practices do not work properly (see, e.g., Nurmi, 1986; Sveiby and Lloyd, 1987; Nurmi et al., 1992; Lehtimäki, 1993; White and Jacques, 1995; Wernerfelt, 1995, for recent debates). People can work in mechanical organiza-

FIGURE 2.6.Two Types of Organizations

	MECHANIC ORGANIZATION	ORGANIC ORGANIZATION
Line of Business	Industry	Knowledge Business
Line of Service	Administration and a Part of Commerce	Personal Service
Values	Material Values	Spiritual Values
Production	Hardware	Software
Scale of Production	Economics of Scale	Small Is Beautiful
Scale of Service	Mass Production	Personal Service
Raw Material	Material	Information
Production Process	Processing of Material	Information Processing
Productivity Improvement	Automation	Creativity
Efficiency	Efficient Throughout	Know-How
Product	Tangible	Intangible
Role of Man	Object	Subject
Product Diversity	Standardization	Customization
Tempo	Synchronization	Differentiation
Organization	Structure	Network
Interaction	Hierarchy	Process
Permanence	Stabile	Labile
Horizontal Cooperation	Departmental	Interpersonal
Vertical Cooperation	Strategic and Operative Levels	Vague
Public Relations	Specialists	As Many as Possible
Organizational Transactions	Exchange Relationships	Vague
Capital	Real Capital	Human Capital

tions for extrinsic rewards only, but it is impossible to create know-how and customer satisfaction without intrinsic interest in what one is doing.

The division of labor is peculiar to an organic organization. Management cannot rely primarily on hierarchy. The line between strategy and operations is transparent once the strategy is built on the knowledge of people. The horizontal division of labor works better by personal interaction than by departmentation. Even the borderline of organization is very fluid. Manifold interfaces and networks (see Baba and Imai, 1993) and barters (see Kreiner and Schultz, 1993) build up a critical mass between people and organizations. After all, knowledge is not given away in exchange, but it stays and grows in the possession of everyone who is taking part in the exchange.

The idea of the virtual corporation is based on the exchange of information between independent units in a corporation (Davidow and Malone, 1992). Establishing a knowledge-intensive company requires more human than real capital. From this, it follows that the control of an organization over its members cannot be as tight as it used to be in traditional organizations. In all, many traditional assumptions on organizing and managing are obsolete in organic organizations.

The fluid organization structure and the professionalism of the personnel tend to make the organic organization conflict-prone. Primarily, conflicts are interpersonal and interdepartmental rather than in the relation between an employer and the employees. Conflicts are an inherent part of this type of organization; they must be tolerated, confronted, and managed, but not suppressed because they are a breeding ground for new ideas.

External or public relations are centralized in traditional organizations. In knowledge-intensive organizations, interfaces and personal networks are built into everyone's job and proficiency. This kind of an interactive and pulsating network cannot be coordinated centrally. Indeed, there will grow a kind of grey zone around the organization with a give-and-take relationship that will continue as long as the participants enrich themselves in the interaction. Organization is then a market of knowledge and learning that excels as long as it can share knowledge with its environment in a profitable way. Organizations comprise a network (Knoke and Kuklinski, 1982) in which each can concentrate on its core competence and buy services that support it from the outside.

Weick (1976, 1979) calls this kind of an organization "loosely coupled." The procedures and ways to work are loosely defined, but the organization is strict in its demand for performance. Persons report different projects to different persons. The most important of them are clients, who judge whether they want to use the services of the organization and its people. Organization is neither a structure nor a collection of rules—it is basically an intricate network of people for people (see Figures 2.7 and 2.8).

There are companies whose success is based on supreme personal service. Even in these companies, human resources are the key resources, and personnel is the strategic core (Grönroos, 1990). The change of persons who serve clients is always perplexing, and it is annoying to reorganize relations with important clients. In the long run, the loss of the "tacit knowledge" embedded in the relations with people can be fatal (Polanyi, 1962). A person is not an interchangeable part of a machine, but the subject of action. Her relations with clients in an organic service organization is more important than her relationship to her superior. This kind of a person can leave her superior and take her clients with her to a competitor or even establish a company of her own. On the other hand, good terms with the superior are not likely to help anyone who collects reclamations from clients.

Figure 2.6 compares organic and mechanical organizations. An organization is contingent with its environment. It is a major task of management to make the organization fit with its environment. This

FIGURE 2.7. Mechanical Organization Structure

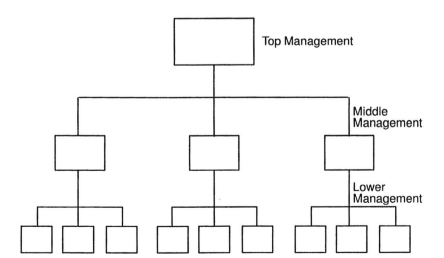

FIGURE 2.8. Organic Processes of Organization

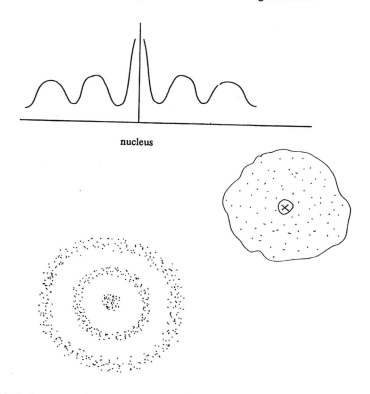

nucleus

This kind of an organization is very fluid. It can be described by the metaphor of wave model developed in nuclear physics.

fit determines the survival of the organization (Pfeffer and Salancik, 1978). Not just any type or form of an organization can survive. Hence, there is only a limited number of types of organizations that are successful as only the fittest survive. Man, in his inventiveness, has experimented with many types of organizations, but only a few of them have survived. Therefore, the number of types has remained limited. Hannan and Freeman (1989) present a Darwinian theory of the population of organizations, their fit, and their survival.

These surviving types have been able to gain an internal equilibrium that fits with the environment. These organizations have adapted to the environment, but they have also influenced the environment. By and large, the environment, the strategy of the organization, and the structure of the organization must be compatible in order for the organization to survive (see Figure 2.9). It is, of course, less difficult for the organization to change its own strategy and structure than its environment; however, it is quite as true that a number of successful organizations have had a great impact on the environment as well.

As the environment, strategy, and structure cannot combine in every way, it follows that only a limited number of types of organizations exist. These types are qualitatively so different from each other that they cannot be compared or measured by the same criteria. They have different systemic qualities.

From this, it is easy to understand that organizational change is never an easy endeavor (see Aaltio-Marjosola, 1991, for one case, and Laughlin, 1991, for a recent account). As the equilibrium of the organization is a survival factor, the organization resists impacts that destabilize the equilibrium. Hence, a transformation cannot succeed one element at a time, stepwise, little by little. These little changes work against the force fields that maintain the equilibrium; thus, such changes are reversed back. The transformation occurs only with a necessary impact on the whole of the organization so that it shifts one

FIGURE 2.9. The Tension of Environment, Strategy, and Organization

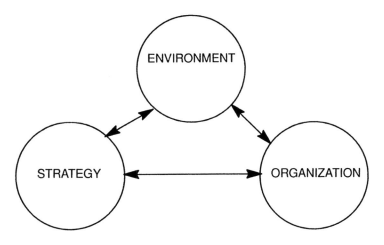

equilibrium to another, creating a new state of equilibrium. This kind of a transformation seldom succeeds without a phase of disequilibrium. Its management varies from difficult to impossible.

Is it possible for a company to survive with an inappropriate organization? It depends on the unique business advantage. With a supreme business advantage—superior products, market leadership—a company can succeed for some time at least in spite of an unfit organization or even with poor management (see Figure 2.10). This is noticeable in monopolies; they need not pay any attention to their internal resources. But monopolies do not live forever. Supreme know-how, competitive advantages, monopolies, and even imperiums collapse. Nothing fails like success. It is by way of management leadership that business advantage is developed or left undeveloped (see Figure 2.11).

FIGURE 2.10. The Emergence of the Type of Organization

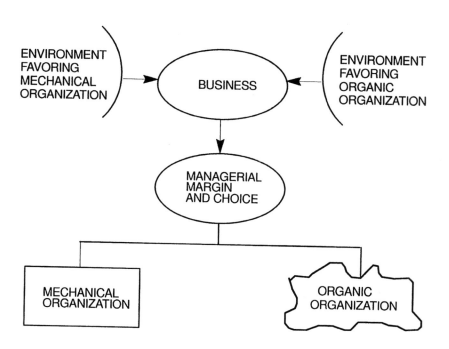

FIGURE 2.11. Two Types of Management

INDUSTRIAL ERA	POST INDUSTRIAL ERA
RIGID, SLOW, REACTIVE	DYNAMIC, FLEXIBLE, ACTIVE
PAST, CONSERVATIVE, PROTECTIONIST	FUTURE RIDING ON CHANGES, LEADING TRANSITION
SHORT TIME-SPAN, LOOKING FOR QUICK PROFITS AND RAPID EFFECTS	LONG TIME-SPAN, CONSIDER THE LONG-TERM EFFECTS
PRODUCT AND QUANTITY ORIENTATION	QUALITY AND SERVICE ORIENTATION
WHAT IS GOOD FOR US IS GOOD FOR OTHERS	WHAT IS GOOD FOR OTHERS IS AN OPPORTUNITY FOR US
MANAGES HIERARCHY AND DEMANDS LOYALTY	LEADS INTERACTION AND CREATES LOYALTY
COMPETES AGAINST OTHERS	LOOKS FOR SYNERGY AND SHARED PROFITS
REWARDS COMPANY MEN	REWARDS INNOVATIVENESS
CONFORMITY REWARDED, PEOPLE DO WHAT IS ASKED, BELIEF IN MANAGEMENT POWER AND OMNISCIENCE	INDIVIDUALISM AND INITIATIVE REWARDED; NETWORKS BUILT ON CREATIVITY, ACTION, RESPONSIBILITY, AND SPONTANEITY
TECHNOCRATIC, NUMERATE	HIGH PERSONAL STANDARDS, PERSONAL DEVELOPMENT
STANDARDS, AVERAGES, UNIT COSTS	HIGH PERSONAL STANDARDS, PERSONAL DEVELOPMENT
EXPLOITATION OF NATURE	LIVING WITH NATURE

REVIEW QUESTIONS

1. List at least five megatrends.

_____

_____

_____

_____

_____

2. What is meant by microculture, macroculture, and core values?

_____

_____

_____

_____

_____

3. What is meant by organic organizations?

_____

_____

_____

_____

_____

4. List five differences of mechanical and organic organizations?

_____

_____

_____

_____

_____

5. How does the business situation affect the organization and management?

_____

_____

LEARNING EXERCISES

1. Look at the trends in Figures 2.1, 2.2, 2.3, and 2.4. How do they affect your company (or a company you know)? Are they threats to its present products and/or markets? Do they create new opportunities? How do they influence its organization and management? Discuss these points in a group.

2. Examine Figure 2.6, which illustrates the differences of mechanical and organic organizations. Think of the organization in point 1 above. Underline the alternative that describes this organization better on each item of Figure 2.6.

    Having done the above, you can assess how organic your organization is. Is this contingent with the demands of today and the future? What kind of changes do you see necessary? Discuss this with someone else.

3. Examine Figure 2.5 and analyze one foreign country (culture) with it item by item. Compare it with your own country. Share your views with someone who is interested in the same country. You might also find it useful to listen to someone else's analysis from another country and present your analysis to someone else who did not analyze the country you did.

Chapter 3

Strategic Management

The quality of a person's life is in direct proportion to a commitment to excellence, regardless of the chosen field of endeavor.

—Vince Lombardi

IN SEARCH OF BUSINESS EXCELLENCE

Companies are established; they live, grow, develop, and flourish. But many of them die, too, because they have not been able to adapt to changes in the environment. Some companies have shown persistent longevity for even hundreds of years. They have shown vitality; they have grown stronger; they have been able to revive and renew themselves through many crises. They have endured because of their capacity to change without losing their core competence like the ones that have died.

Business and management are long-term endeavors. Companies must be profitable in the short term in order that they can develop resources to be invested in their future. They cannot survive without some kind of a vision of the future. This vision (which may include recognition of comparative advantage and focus of the business) and its changing fit with the opportunities and threats of the environment, can be called strategy (Bettis and Prahalad, 1995). Strategy is a concept having many interpretations and interpretors. According to Mintzberg (1987), strategy has been conceptualized in business literature as a plan, ploy, pattern, position, or perspective. This chapter focuses on strategic management; for those interested in the whole field of corporate strategy, Johnson and Scholes (1993) is recommended.

FIGURE 3.1. Characteristics of Excellent Companies

- A Bias Toward Action
- Simple Form, Lean Staff
- Continued Contact with Customers
- Productivity Improvement Via People
- Operational Autonomy
- Stress on One Key Business Value
- Emphasis on What They Know Best
- Simultaneous Loose-Tight Control

Source: Peters and Waterman (1982, pp. 13-16).

The prediction of the future has turned out to be most unreliable. Plans do not always work out either. Therefore, long-range planning has lost supporters (see Hahn, 1991 and Stumpf and Muellen, 1991). At the very least, its goals cannot be as precise as what was thought in the heyday of the planning approach to strategy. The title of Ansoff, Declerck, and Hayes' 1976 book *From Strategic Planning to Strategic Management* illustrates the change in thinking and practice. Strategic management—seeing, being, going, and influencing the future—has replaced detailed plans.

One way of looking at strategy is to ask what brings business success. This is what Peters and Waterman did in 1982 (also see Darling, 1992). Their book *In Search of Excellence* was a bestseller, but it was also criticized by some (see Aupperle, Acar, and Booth, 1986). The list in Figure 3.1 is based on research about successful American companies. Critics pointed out that many of the companies in Peters and Waterman's sample are not that successful any longer and that they were successful only because they operated in flourishing industries at the time the research was conducted. Besides, the measurement of success is also highly debatable (see Grönhaug and Falkenberg, 1990). With its limitations, the list by Peters and Waterman is worth reading and considering. Even though the items are not universally valid, they are worth discussing in any company. It is useful to raise questions such as the following:

Are the items paid attention to? Are they pertinent to this particular company? Should greater attention be paid to each of them? These lists do not work by way of copying, but by way of company-specific discussion. This is made most useful by benchmarking, which is a methodology by which it is possible to compare the performance of a company to other companies (see Spendolini, 1992, for a comprehensive treatise).

KEYS TO ORGANIZATIONAL EXCELLENCE

The keys to excellence now and in the future for the international firm have been well documented in the contemporary literature (Peters and Austin, 1985; Peters and Waterman, 1982). Whether the organization is large or small, broad-based in several market segments or only a few, there are three primary ways by which it can continue to reflect a commitment to excellence over the long term. The organization must first take good care of its customers via superior product quality and exceptional service. The organization must also constantly innovate. These are basic to achieving long-term superior performance and to sustaining a strategic competitive market advantage.*

These two keys—care of customers and constant innovation—obviously do not constitute all that is needed for the international firm. Solid accounting and financial controls are essential. Organizations that do not have them will fail. Good planning is certainly no luxury, but a necessity. Moreover, business firms can be temporarily or permanently set back by external forces, such as an overvalued currency or the loss of access to needed resources. Nevertheless, these other factors are seldom, if ever, the basis for lasting distinction. That is, financial control is vital, but the firm does not sell financial control: It sells a quality product or service. The firm seldom sustains superior performance through mere access to resources; it sustains this through innovativeness in resource acquisition and use, and subsequent market development. The firm may be affected by an overvalued currency, but it sustains performance by

---

*The material in the next three sections is based on Darling and Nurmi (1995).

adding enough innovative value to the product or service that it is profitably salable despite monetary variability.

In reality, neither superior care of customers nor constant innovation—two of the three cutting edges and sustaining aspects of excellence in today's successful international organization—is built upon managerial genius, unusual operational techniques, or mystical strategic moves or countermoves in the marketplace. Both are built, instead, on the existence of people whose commitment evolves from an established and solid foundation of listening, trust, and respect for the dignity and the creative potential of each person in the organization (see Figure 3.2). This foundation facilitates the establishment of a "winning team" of people committed to the achievement of the firm's goals and objectives for excellence. Such a group thereby becomes a team when each member is instilled with such individual confidence and pride in his or her contribution that praise can be readily given to the abilities of others and the total performance of the group can excel.

Most international business firms that have been successful in creating an excellent workplace culture have done so not by their cleverness, but by the fact that each and every aspect of the business is better than average. So the keys to organizational quality in a firm

FIGURE 3.2. Model of Keys to Organizational Excellence

focus on three variables—care of customers, constant innovation, and committed people. Yet in this model of excellence, something is still missing—that *one* element that connects *all* the others. As noted in Figure 3.2, that one element is effective managerial leadership. Through the development and implementation of leadership strategies, the manager helps to facilitate the reflection of excellence in the organization (Peters and Austin, 1985).

MANAGEMENT VERSUS LEADERSHIP

The primary factor that has prevented the creation of a culture of excellence in many international business firms is that they have tended to be overmanaged and underled. Managers in these organizations may excel in the ability to handle the daily routine, yet never question whether the routine should be done at all. In this regard, there is a profound difference between management and leadership, but one should readily recognize that both are important. To "manage" means to bring about, to accomplish, to have charge of or responsibility for, and to conduct. Leading is influencing, guiding in direction, course, action, and opinion. The distinction is crucial. Managers are people who do things right, and leaders are people who do the right things. The difference may be summarized as activities of vision and judgment, which facilitate effectiveness as a leader, versus activities of mastering routines, which facilitate efficiency as a manager.

Thus, the degree to which managers are also leaders relates to how they construe their roles. Those who are successful view themselves as leaders, not just managers. That is to say, they concern themselves with their organizations' dimensions of excellence in all respects. Their perspective is vision oriented (Bennis and Nanus, 1985). They do not limit their attention to the "how to's," the proverbial "nuts and bolts," but include the parameters of action, the "doing the right things," particularly as those things relate to the care of customers, the cultivation of innovation, and the nurturing and development of committed people in the organization. A real test of successful leadership in international management today lies in giving, to the greatest extent possible, opportunities to others in the situational context of the firm. One does not have to be brilliant to be a good leader, but one does have to understand other people—how they feel, what makes them tick, and the most effective ways to influence them. For example, consider the following facts. In many studies of leadership in international business, it has been shown that the average executive spends most of the working day dealing with people. The largest single cost in most businesses is people. The biggest, most valuable asset any company usually has is its people. All management plans for enhancement are carried out, or fail to be carried out, by people.

SUCCESSFUL LEADERSHIP STRATEGIES

A leader in management is a person who inspires, by appropriate means, sufficient competence to influence a group of individuals to become willing followers in the achievement of organizational goals. Four key strategies are of primary importance: (1) attention through vision; (2) meaning through communication; (3) trust through positioning; and (4) confidence through respect, as shown in Figure 3.3 (Bennis and Nanus, 1985).

Attention Through Vision

The management of attention through vision helps to create a focus for the organization. Each manager is expected to carry out assigned functions and responsibilities in an organization, but successful leaders in international management today do more than that. They are acutely aware that everything related to their responsibilities and the functions of their organization might be done faster, better, more reliably, with fewer errors, and at a lower cost. These are the drumbeats to which they march (Bennis, 1989). They carry them constantly in mind, looking for and considering many possible answers. They are continually looking for problems rather than merely solving the problems that come their way. They are creative change agents because they want to find a better way and really work to achieve it.

Henry David Thoreau described the concept of vision when he wrote: "If a man does not keep pace with his companions, perhaps it is because he hears a different drummer. Let him step to the music which he hears, however measured or far away." Perhaps it is the

FIGURE 3.3. Model of Keys to Organizational Excellence and Leadership Strategies

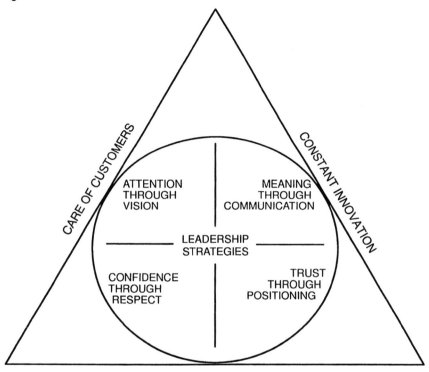

COMMITTED PEOPLE

beat of the drum that separates the successful from the unsuccessful. Perhaps it is the price that the successful leader in management has agreed to pay. Happy are the leaders who can free themselves to dream dreams and are then ready to pay the price to bring these dreams to fruition. Or said another way, when one has agreed upon the price that she must pay for success in the managerial leadership dimension, it enables her to forget the price.

The new leaders in international management have an agenda, an unparalleled concern with outcomes. These leaders are results-oriented individuals, and results get attention. Their visions or intentions are compelling and pull people toward them like a gigantic magnet. This visionary intensity, coupled with commitment, is exciting and contagious. These intense personalities do not have to coerce people to pay attention: they are so intent on what they are doing that, like a person enthusiastically absorbed in operating a new personal computer, they draw others in. Vision grabs attention! Initially, it grabs the leader, and management of attention encourages others to make a commitment to organizational achievement.

Robert Kennedy made it popular, but George Bernard Shaw said it long ago: "Some see things as they are, and ask, why? I prefer to see things as they might be, and ask, why not?" Successful leaders in international management are looking at what they consider to be their vision and the possibilities of what their organizations can become, and having done this, they are committing themselves and their firms to the discipline that is necessary to make these visions a reality.

Meaning Through Communication

Among different international organizations, there are many interesting and exciting visions and noble intentions. Many managers have important and very meaningful objectives, but without effective communication, very little will be realized. Success in managerial leadership requires the capacity to relate a compelling image of a desired state of affairs—the kind of image that induces enthusiasm and commitment in others. The management of meaning, focusing on a mastery of communication, is inseparable from effective leadership and organizational excellence today.

There are a number of issues relating to effective communication. First, an organization depends on the existence of shared meanings and interpretations of reality, which facilitate coordinated action. Leaders articulate and define what may previously have remained implicit or unsaid; then they create perspectives that provide a focus for new attention. By so doing, they consolidate or challenge prevailing wisdom. In short, an essential factor in leadership is the capacity to influence and organize meaning for the personnel of the international business firm (Bennis and Nanus, 1985).

The second thing to keep in mind is that the methods by which leaders convey and shape meaning vary enormously. Although such meanings may vary in style and may be verbal or nonverbal, every successful leader is aware that an organization is based on a set of shared meanings that define roles and authority, procedures, and objectives. Finally, what is meant by the creation of meaning goes beyond what is usually meant by communication, and focuses on more than facts or even knowledge. Facts and knowledge concern technique, methodology, and knowing how to do things. The distinctive role of leadership is the quest for the know-why ahead of the know-how. Managers, for the most part, deal with a process known as problem solving. Leadership involves the form of discovery known as problem *finding*. This is another difference between managers and leaders: It focuses on the contrast between routine problem solvers and problem finders in the business arena.

Communication creates meaning for people in the organization, or at least it should. It is a primary way in which any group of individuals, small or large, can become aligned behind the overarching goals of the organization. Getting the correct and intended message across at every level is an important key. Basically, it is what the creative process is all about and what, once again, helps to separate managers from leaders. Another important aspect of communication is empathy. Successful leaders are open and sensitive to the needs and differences of others and look at relative viewpoints rather than absolutes. Empathy is understanding that birthplace, political belief, gender, financial status, education, and intelligence are not measures of worth. The pathway to effective communication is accepting the fact that every human being is a distinct and unique individual. This is at the heart of nurturing the foundation of committed people in the international firm of today.

Trust Through Positioning

Trust is a facilitator that helps to make it possible for an organization to function effectively. It is difficult to imagine an excellence-oriented team that lacks a reasonable degree of trust and credibility. An organization without trust is more than an anomaly; it is a misnomer. Trust implies accountability, predictability, and reliability. It is what sells products and keeps organizations operating. Trust provides the foundation that maintains organizational integrity. We know when it is present and when it is not; we know that it is essential and that it is based on predictability. The truth is that we trust people who are predictable, whose positions are known and have continuity. Leaders who are trusted make themselves known and make their positions clear.

Positioning encompasses the set of actions necessary to implement the vision of the leader. If vision is the idea, then positioning is the niche the leader establishes. For this niche to be achieved, the leader in management today must be a reflection not only of clarity, but of constancy, of persistence, of reliability (Bennis and Nanus, 1985). Through establishing the position—and, more important, maintaining continuity—the leader establishes trust. Persistence does not always mean pursuing the same thing forever. It does mean giving full concentration and effort to whatever one is doing. It means doing the tough things first and looking downstream for gratification and rewards. It means working longer hours, going more miles, filling the day with full measure, and always being on the lookout for a better way of fulfilling one's responsibilities.

Integrity, reflected in honesty and frankness properly clothed in tact, is a key to the process of establishing trust through positioning. Words associated with integrity are themselves interesting: the quality of being complete, unimpaired, moral soundness, honesty, freedom from corrupting influence or practice, predictable strictness in the fulfilment of contracts and the discharge of trusts. There is no greater need in managerial leaders than the need for integrity (Bennis, 1989), for being true to trust, reflecting the fact that the whole substance of things can be seen from the "top of the table." And this is not something that new policies will fix, or new rules or regulations will establish, for ingenious individuals will always find ways to circumvent both policies and regulations. Integrity is simply something that a person is in him or herself. It is, in a sense, the assurance that what one sees, what is said to be, is something that can be counted on, without qualification. Integrity in the leadership position leads to trust in those individuals counted on to facilitate achievement of excellence in the operations of the organization.

Confidence Through Respect

A key factor in building confidence through respect focuses on the creative deployment of self. The creative deployment of self makes managerial leadership a deeply personal activity because of the necessity of positive self-regard. A positive self-regard does not focus on self-importance or egotistic self-centeredness. There is no trace of self-worship in managerial leaders, but they know their worth. They trust themselves without letting their ego or image get in the way. A positive self-regard seems to consist of three major components: knowledge of one's own strengths; the capacity to nurture and develop those strengths; and the ability to discern the fit between one's strengths and weaknesses and the organization's needs (Bennis and Nanus, 1985). Such leaders are acutely aware of their strengths and are continually involved in developing them further.

International managerial leaders who have a high degree of respect function out of the OK mode of existence—that is, I'm OK and you're OK, too. These leaders are often able to bring out the best results in others through the inducement of a positive other-regard in their colleagues and employees. They see latent talent and encourage it; they listen to those around them and they realize that a person's inability to do one job does not mean that the individual is incompetent in all jobs. The creation of confidence through respect thereby becomes contagious throughout the organization.

"The greatest discovery of my generation," wrote William James, "is that human beings can alter their lives by altering their attitudes of mind." Respect is based upon the internalization of value. The verb "to respect" means "to appreciate the value of." In the human being, respect is a major characteristic of successful leadership. It provides the basis for one's ability to appreciate oneself and others genuinely, and to accomplish worthy goals and success for the organization.

But sometimes, nothing fails like success. Success is apt to blind managers from seeing threats. Or it may cause a company to stick to the formula on which the success was based long after the formula grew obsolete. Success sows seeds of failure. This is clearly shown by Slatter (1984), O'Toole (1985), and Arogyaswami, Barker, and Yasai-Adekani (1995), who followed up the stories of companies that were excellent once. Potts and Behr (1987) continued from this and studied companies that have been turned around. Their sample consisted of managers who had been able to turn around a mismanaged company. From this they were able to generalize the following conclusions:

- Anticipate changes in competition and be prepared to react to them quickly.
- Know your strengths and build on them.
- Remember that technology and know-how are driving forces
- Develop strategic alliances.
- Create partnerships.
- Take calculated risks and develop intrapreneurship.
- Management is not enough in the future—leadership and visionaries are needed.
- Create a balance between the necessities of today and the requirements of tomorrow.

APPROACHES TO STRATEGY

There is an abundance of schools of strategy. Näsi (1991a,b) gives an excellent review of them. In what follows, some of the most influential ones are discussed, with a special emphasis on the implementation of the strategy.

Igor Ansoff can be called the first guru of strategy. He conceptualized strategy as a product-market mix in 1965. There are basically four product-market strategies as illustrated in Figure 3.4:

1. A company can penetrate into its present mix.
2. It can develop or acquire new products for its present market.
3. It can conquer new markets for its present products.
4. It can diversify into new product-market areas.

The last option has turned out to be difficult. In order for it to succeed at all, there needs to be a synergy between the present mix and the new mix created in the diversification. Synergy means that the interaction of the company and its new product-market mix must produce more than the sum of the combination of the two (the 1+1=3 effect).

Porter's (1980) so-called generic strategies (Figure 3.5) comprise one of the best-known strategy formulations of today. The generic strategies are the three fundamental ways in which a company can gain a sustainable competitive advantage:

1. In *cost leadership strategy*, the company is the low-cost producer in its industry. The competitive advantage is based on price competition in the market.

2. In *differentiation strategy,* the company is unique in its industry as regards characteristics that the clients find important in
their decisions to buy.
3. In *focus strategy,* the company chooses some segments of the
industry and tailors its strategy to these segments only.

Focusing may be based on costs or on differentiation. Cost leadership strategy tends to lead to a mechanical organization, while
differentiation breeds a more organic organization. Porter argues
that firms had better choose one of these basic strategies and that
sticking in the middle will not work. Nonetheless, there are companies that started with a new product and with a differentiation strategy, but as new competitors entered the market they benefited from
their learning curve and became cost leaders in their chosen seg-
ment (see Figure 3.5).
Porter's argument works best in mature, competitive industries. In
line with this, Porter even presents barriers to entry and other defensive means by which a company can maintain the position it has
achieved. His formulation can be characterized as an industry strategy and as a competitive strategy. Economists tend to see competitive advantage as a matter of cost competitiveness. Competitive
advantage can, however, be built on superior know-how, know-why
of customer needs, management skills, products, logistics, and other

FIGURE 3.4. Product-Market Strategy Alternatives According to Ansoff

PRODUCTS / MARKETS	PRESENT	NEW
PRESENT	PENETRATION	PRODUCT DEVELOPMENT
NEW	MARKETING	DIVERSIFICATION

FIGURE 3.5. Three Generic Strategies

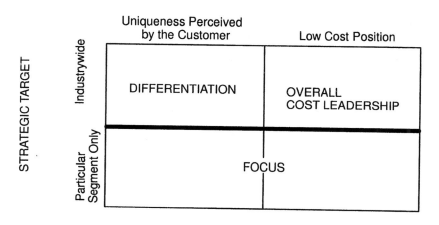

Source: Porter (1980).

core competences. Knowledge can create leverage and creative use of scarce resources (Hamel and Prahalad, 1993; Burton, 1995). In emerging industries, in knowledge-intensive business, and in many services, the strategy can be, however, much more assertive, innovative, even aggressive than Porter's generic strategies imply. This can take place by innovating new products and services and by conquering new markets or by combining the two. Even then, a strategy is needed to focus and to set priorities as it is impossible to gain superiority with limited resources in many fields. "Busyness" alone does not create business.

Portfolio analyses came into vogue in the 1980s in the hands of financial analysts and financial strategists in particular. The Boston matrix seen in Figure 3.6 (Hedley, 1977) is, no doubt, the most widely used portfolio analysis. It analyzes and categorizes strategic business units into the following four categories on the basis of relative market share and growth:

1. When the market share and growth are positive, the unit is a star and a target of investment.

2. When both are sluggish, the unit is called a dog, and it is a target for divestment or liquidation.
3. When the market share is high, but the growth is sluggish, the unit is a cash cow.
4. When the growth is high, but the market share is a modest one, the unit is called a question mark, and a further analysis of competition and competitors is needed

FIGURE 3.6. The Boston Matrix

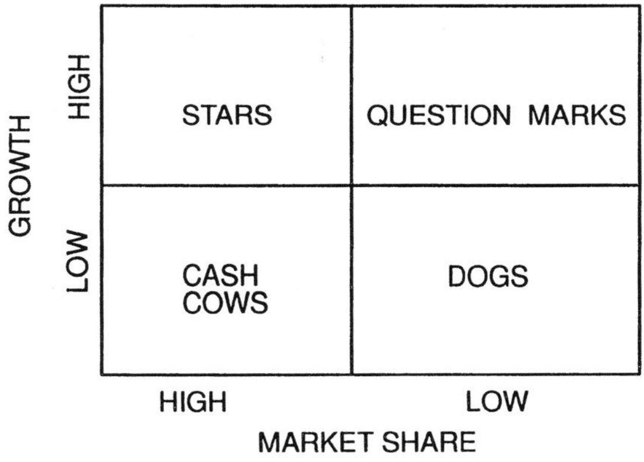

The optimal cash-flow runs from the cash cows to the stars. This kind of a portfolio analysis is best as a financial strategic tool of diversified companies, in which the headquarters' involvement in the units is limited to financial strategy and control. It may, on the other hand, be too crude of an analysis. A further analysis of question marks or even dogs may show that they can be turned around into a positive trajectory by an appropriate management. Indeed, the depression in Western Europe and the United States in the first part of 1990s has been attributed to too much financial management and too little management of business and productivity at the plant and shop level.

Torger Reve (1990) has argued for a strategy formulation based on transaction cost theory. One of its merits is that it enables us to discern:

- which are the core, strategic functions of a company that it must cherish and develop under its own auspices;
- which functions it can secure by means of strategic alliances with other companies;
- which of its functions it can buy from the market; and
- which of its present functions it can neglect or axe without essential loss to its business.

The strategic core consists of the resources of the company that are specific to the company, that are its raison d'etre. They may be physical like location, investments, etc., but more often and what is more important, they may be intangible core competences (Prahalad and Hamel, 1990) and outcomes of organizational learning. They are not just technical skills, but what is more important, skills to work together in the company, with the clients and the markets. This kind of "tacit knowledge" (Polanyi, 1962) takes time to develop, and once it is lost, its rebuilding is costly, difficult, or even impossible (Nonaka, 1991). Therefore, it should be specially cherished even in organizational reshuffles.

In a developed economy of business networks of suppliers, a company should focus and concentrate its resources on what it is best at. It is arduous enough to develop the strategic core and core competences. Therefore, a company can leave the rest to others and buy services instead of trying to make everything itself (see Rubin, 1990, pp. 3–46). Knowing its strategic core, a company can have the following four basic business strategies (Figure 3.7):

1. A company can gain economics of scale with a bigger market share at the cost of its competitors.
2. It can diversify into new businesses and/or partners that have synergy with the strategic core. Diversification is known to be a difficult strategy, and it has so often failed just because the company has lost sight of its strategic core instead of building on it—for instance, a forest company diversified into high-tech measurement devices because the latter looked like a promising industry.
3. It is possible to secure subcontractors and raw materials by joining with the suppliers.

4. The last direction of a strategic alliance is with distributors, which increases the control of marketing to the clients.

All four strengthen the strategic core and are accordingly proper strategic alliances, whatever form they may take.

The growth of a company tends to create management problems, and it always implies business risks as well, but it is sometimes necessary, notwithstanding. There are grow or die circumstances. Keeping the strategic core in mind helps to avoid unmanageable growth into areas that create more problems than they solve. A good "bad" example is provided by some knowledge-intensive companies that as a result of unforeseen profitability in their own business invested in real estate. This, however, took the time and

FIGURE 3.7. Integrated Model of Strategic Management

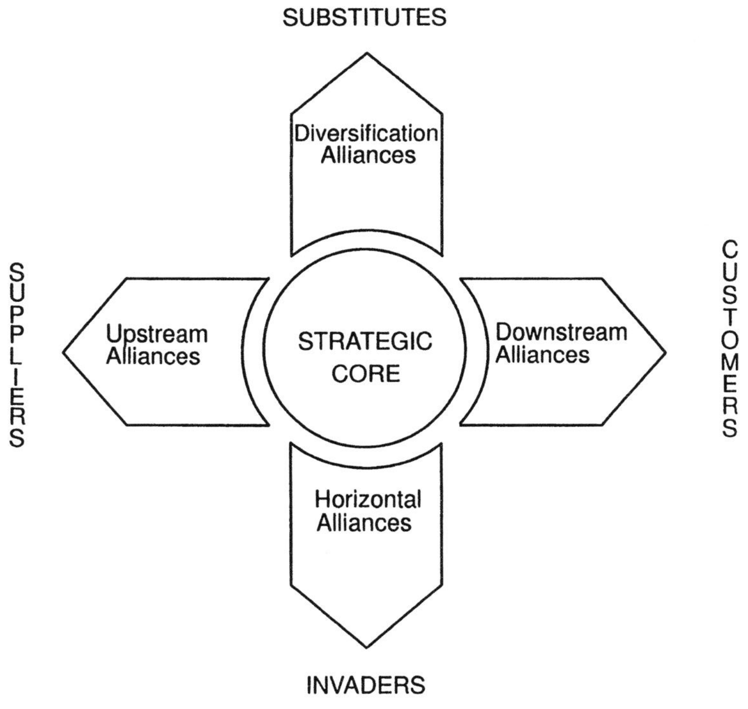

Source: Adapted from Reve (1991).

concentration ability of the managers away from the core competences of the business with the consequence that both the knowledge business and real estate began to perform poorly. However, the
companies in the same business that invested in human resources
and know-how sailed better through changing business tides.

Strategic matters are the responsibility of top management, and
they belong on the agenda of board meetings as well. To be able to
carry through the strategies, the top management needs to educate
the personnel in strategic thinking. Actually, in a number of businesses, the strategic impulses come from below and even from
operative, professional persons (Viitanen, 1993). A strategy does
not live on paper nor in the corridors of the building. Strategies
become reality in everyday action. In other words, strategic thinking should be a part and parcel of the corporate culture, the day-to-
day interaction and partnership of the organization. Much too often
strategies are happily forgotten after they have been developed in a
complicated and cumbersome formal process.

One more way of saying this is that strategic goals are an essence
of corporate culture. Harju (1981) showed that a planning attitude
correlates more positively with profitability than developments in
planning methods. Denison's (1985) research results seem to indicate that the ideals that the personnel subscribes to may have a more
positive correlation with performance than their behavior as such
has. As intangible as this may sound, this kind of a culture can be
influenced by way of management and training (Nurmi, 1976).

The gap between the strategy and the operations is noticeable in
many companies (Waldersee and Sheather, 1996; Barney and Zajac,
1994). The strategy remains on the paper on which it was written,
whereas the operations are influenced by momentary pushes, political power-games, defenses, constraints, and resistance to change
(Figure 3.8). The intentions and action remain loosely coupled, in
the words of Weick (1976). Most literature on strategy concerns its
planning, while what happens after the strategy has been fixed is
much less researched. Mintzberg and Waters (1985) observed that
strategies often emerge irrespective of what was intended to be the
strategy. In a vertical organization structure with many levels, the
strategy designed on the top may never flow down to the operations
the way the strategists might like to think. Often the headquarters'

FIGURE 3.8. Two Phases of Strategy: Planning and Implementation

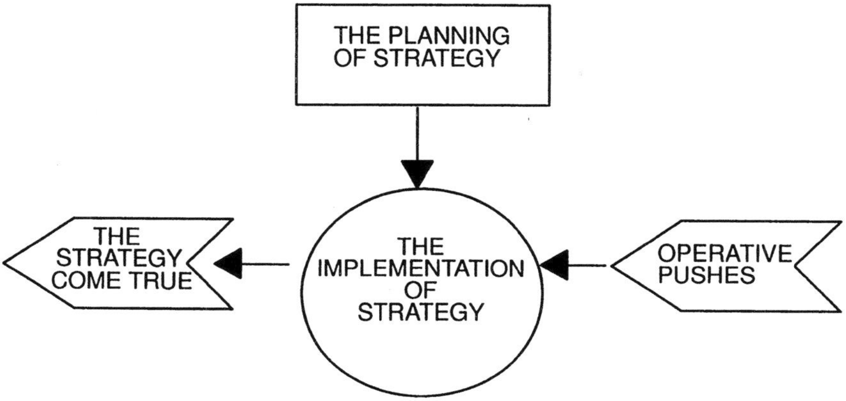

managers limit themselves to financial strategy and control only, leaving the business strategies to the units (see Goold and Campbell,1987, for a detailed analysis). In some cases, strategies have a symbolic meaning without intended business linkage (Broms and Gahmberg, 1979). Though all this may serve some purpose, it would be better if the strategy and operations would go hand in hand. In order to attain this, the design of strategy itself should not be separated from operative considerations (Figure 3.9).

SWOT-analysis is a good case to illustrate the previous discussion. Strategy making usually contains an analysis of internal Strengths and Weaknesses and external Opportunities and Threats—hence, the acronym SWOT. The point is to build the strategy on the internal strengths and external opportunities; where the two meet makes up a comparative competitive advantage of the company. The weaknesses must be known either to mend them or—and this is often a cheaper solution—to select a strategy where the weaknesses do not matter. Threats are easiest to avoid when seen early enough and as weak signals.

There are sophisticated, elegant, and comprehensive techniques for SWOT-analysis (see, e.g., Handscombe and Norman, 1989). They have produced voluminous and lucid reports. But it just so happens that management seldom finds the time for these kinds of elaborate analyses, and without top management commitment, little strategic

FIGURE 3.9. Overlapping Strategy and Operations

change will come out of the exercise. The result may be a paralysis by analysis (Lenz and Lyles, 1985).

Figures 3.10 and 3.11 show results of a quick SWOT. It was conducted in a training session of the management team of a company. The team first discussed the threats of the company, then estimated the fatality and probability of each, and determined the relative order of the threats. The opportunities were spotted in the same way. Later the same day, the debate continued about seizing the strengths and opportunities and circumventing the weaknesses and threats. As a consequence, the participants were committed to what had been discussed, and these strategic considerations became a part of their thinking and job behavior.

It is interesting and useful to read about excellence and strategies, but none of them work by way of copying. None of them releases management from strategic thinking and strategic responsibility. Organized strategic thinking is an outcome of strategic talks and broad interaction in the organization. The process of interaction is as important as its quickly changing outcomes. This organizational

FIGURE 3.10. Threats of a Forest Company

THREATS	PROB-ABILITY	FATAL-ITY	EXPECT-ANCY	ACTION
1. Government policy	.42	.80	.34	Lobbying, liaison with employer's association
2. Shortage of capital	.35	.75	.26	Issue of stocks, liquidity planning
3. Shortage of raw material	.42	.62	.26	Recycling, purchase of forests, joint purchasing ventures
4. Misinvestments	.25	1.00	.25	Focused business strategy, management selection and training
5. Shortage of labor	.65	.37	.24	Active personnel policy, rationalization, liaison with the township officials

learning brings forth a better preparation for the future than fore-casts, plans, goals, or strategies on paper can ever do. Organizational learning breeds shared organizational values and around them an ability to be resilient on encountering surprises and shocks that changes in the environment inevitably provide.

Strategic planning has given way to strategic management. It is now time for strategic management to give way to organizational strategic learning (Goddard and Houlder, 1995; Wick and Leon, 1995). By way of strategic learning, the borderline of the company and its environment is no longer a buffer to defend the organization from pushes, but a scanner to search opportunities from the environment.

Strategic organizational learning needs strategic leadership. The concept of strategy has approached leadership research (Schendel, 1989), and the concept of strategic leadership has emerged (Bennis, 1989). Strategic leadership means that:

FIGURE 3.11. Operations of a Forest Company

OPPORTUNITIES	PROB-ABILITY-	UTILITY	EXPECT-ANCY	ACTION
1. Improvement of the value added	.93	.90	.84	Plant planning project
2. The increase of capacity	.93	.55	.51	Plant planning project, acquisition of new machinery, shift work
3. New lines of business	.75	.48	.36	Feasibility study
4. Rationalization	.48	.43	.21	Plant planning project, logistic planning
5. Growth of demand	.50	.40	.20	Search of new markets in the Mediterranean area

- doing the right things is more important than doing things right;
- what is done is more important than how it is done;
- management builds on what is unique, strong, and powerful in the organization (i.e., on comparative advantages and sharing instead of dividing to gain governance);
- responsibility for future priorities is more important than political struggle for power;
- there is a continuous debate on what lies on the horizon, while planning for the next year is a matter of routine;
- form follows purpose and not the other way around;
- people weigh more than hierarchy, systems, and political machinery; and
- people are trusted and listened to instead of being controlled.

This is idealism, some may say. Very true! But it is quite as true that the leaders of the future need idealism without illusions and realism without cynicism, as John F. Kennedy declared in one of his speeches.

REVIEW QUESTIONS

1. What are the keys to organizational excellence? Discuss.

2. What are the leadership strategies? Discuss.

3. What are Porter's generic strategies? Discuss.

4. Discuss the Boston matrix as an example of a portfolio.

5. Discuss designing and implementing as dimensions of strategy formulation.

7. What is meant by strategic leadership? How does this differ from strategic management?

LEARNING EXERCISES

Analyze your company (or any company that you know) by ranking its threats and opportunities.

Threats

Think that five years have passed from this day, your company faces the possibility of bankruptcy. What reasons could lead to the bankruptcy? List them in the first column of Figure 3.12.

Assess the probability of each of the reasons for the bankruptcy. Use the scale 0.0 to 1.0. If you think that the reason is impossible, give it the value 0.0. If you think it is certain, give the value 1.0. Use any value between 0.0 and 1.0. Obviously, the reasons that you listed have a probability somewhere between the two extremes. A reason that you would give the value 0.8 has, then, a greater probability of occurrence than a reason that you give the value 0.4. Write down your probability assessment in the second column of Figure 3.2 corresponding to the reason for bankruptcy that you listed in column 1.

Now assess the fatality of each reason on the scale 0.0–1.0. The value 0.0 implies that the reason is not fatal at all to the company, and the value 1.0 implies an immediate bankruptcy. Use any value between 0.0–1.0 to reflect your assessment of fatality. Write your assessments in the third column of Figure 3.12.

Next, multiply the probability of the fatality of each reason and place the result in the fourth column of Figure 3.12. Now, you have the ranked order of the threats of the company in the fourth column.

Finally, think what can be done to prevent the threat from coming true, and write your ideas down in the last column of Figure 3.12.

Opportunities

Think that five years have passed from this day, and your company is now extraordinarily successful. What reasons could have led to this success. List them in the first column of Figure 3.13.

Assess the probability and value of each of the reasons. Use the scale from 0.0 to 1.0 so that the value 0.0 would imply no probability or utility at all, whereas 1.0 would mean a high probability of an immediate boost for success. Write your assessments in the second and third columns of Figure 3.13.

Next, multiply the probability and the utility of each reason and place the results in the fourth column of Figure 3.13 to show the rank order of the opportunities of the company.

Finally, think about what can be done to seize the opportunities, and then write down your ideas in the final column.

FIGURE 3.12. Analysis of Threats to a Company

THREATS	PROBABILITY P	FATALITY F	P X F	ACTION
1.				
2.				
3.				
4.				
5.				

FIGURE 3.13. Analysis of Opportunities for a Company

OPPORTUNITIES	PROBABILITY P	UTILITY U	P X U	ACTION
1.				
2.				
3.				
4.				
5.				

Chapter 4

Operative Management

*Some see things as they are, and ask why. I prefer to see
things as they might be, and ask why not.*

—George Bernard Shaw

MANAGEMENT AS A JOB, POSITION, AND RESPONSIBILITY

Managers are appointed. Managers are expected to decide and be responsible for decisions and achieve what has been agreed upon with the help of other people. Management is a job, an office, a position, a status, and a responsibility that is visible in the title of the managerial job. Along with the appointment, the manager receives social tokens of the position: the responsibility, duty, and possibility to influence her domain and the people in it. The appointment does not automatically give authority, and even if it gives it, the authority must be earned and re-earned on the job. Managers can be appointed, but leadership must be earned.

This chapter deals with operational management. It views managerial work as a position and responsibility, and deals with managerial roles or expectations that are attached to managerial positions. Activities relating to operative management, including such issues as organizing as a key managerial function, management by objectives, and maintaining positive relationships between superiors and subordinates are discussed in Chapter 5.

There are textbooks that describe management as a systematic, well-planned, professional activity, or, at least, these texts try to teach management to behave that way. These books would seem to claim that, if some managers do not behave this way, they exemplify poor management practice. The term "scientific management" seems to indicate that management can be seen as a decision-making methodology with its own professional techniques, methods, and systems in the same way as, say, a dentist uses professional education and methods to diagnose and cure dental problems.

Now, however, a host of research observations (e.g., Carlson, 1951; Mintzberg, 1973; Nurmi, 1983) have been accumulated to support the everyday observation that managers do not behave as systematic decision makers at all. This holds true of executives who are known for excellent managerial and business performance. Instead, brevity, variety, fragmentation, unrelentless pace, interruptions, superficiality, muddles, and messes are "the nature of managerial work" to quote the title of Mintzberg's (1973) book that became a classic in the field in less than a decade.

Managerial work does not consist of well-defined issues that would easily render themselves to analytical techniques or systematic planning. Instead, issues are complicated webs and jumbles; even the outline and definition of managerial issues are far from clear-cut. Companies and managers do have strategies, and they may be quite obliging. However, the link between strategies and the daily managerial work is not a straight line. It may not be conscious even to the managers themselves. The strategy in the back of the mind of a manager is more potent than the one on paper, and the latter cannot keep pace with developments in the former.

It is impossible to catalog managerial tasks one by one because tasks constantly change. A manager is in charge of his job as a responsibility. This is a short and comprehensive managerial job description. It is up to a manager to decide what this responsibility demands in a given situation, and situations vary in an unforeseen and discontinuous manner. Managers cannot have fixed working hours. If, for example, an important client wants to see him after normal working hours, he cannot afford to respond that it is after his working hours nor even to ask extra salary for the time spent for overtime. Managers are not paid for the time nor other personal input in the job, but for the output or performance in the job. A manager's job security varies between poor and nonexistent. A poor performance of a manager affects so many people and things that it is better to remove the manager than let the rest suffer. Managerial work is measured by performance—the performance of the people and other resources of which he is in charge. A manager does not measure his own performance; it is measured by others. There are measures provided by accounting and other forms of information technology, but it is the rapport he has with the others that counts in the end. The manager's superior is usually the most influential of these others.

Management and manager refer to a position in an organization. Position is attached to power and responsibility. The two are ambiguous concepts, partly because they are laden with affective and political connotations. Power is often personified. He has got power; the others have not. But in a closer scrutiny, the power of persons is attached to the position they hold. The managing director has in his position more possibilities to influence, i.e., position power, than the operative people have irrespective of how skillful power players they are as persons. The managing director can, with his poor performance, drive the whole company into the red, whereas its operative persons cannot do as much harm—at least without a collective action. A managing director has little chance to do little mistakes, as his mistakes tend to always have larger repercussions. On the other hand, the power in the position of a managing director is attached to a great responsibility. Responsibility and power go together; there cannot be one without the other. Power without responsibility means tyranny; responsibility without power is most frustrating, even suffocating. The balance between the two is seldom perfect in the imperfect world of humans. But too great an imbalance has hideous consequences.

Theorists in fields as diverse as theology, ethics, law, politics, and organization theory have written disciplined treatises on power and responsibility. In managerial practice, organizational responsibility is part and parcel of what managers do or fail to do. Management is responsibility instead of a collection of individual tasks.

A manager can, and he needs to, delegate tasks for those who report to him because his responsibility implies more work than he himself can do. Delegating as much as he can, a manager can focus and put his own effort on the most important tasks without using his precious time on the less important ones. This sounds fair and simple. In practice, it is seldom either.

There are managers who are unwilling to delegate because they are afraid that by so doing they will lose their power and authority. If a manager keeps all the information, decisions, and power to himself, he may believe that he secures his own position and prevents his subordinates from advancing abreast of or even past him. This, of course, has a negative influence on performance, efficiency, and effectiveness. In the long run, it does not even secure anyone's power nor possibilities to influence, but it is the performance that counts.

"I have never had as much power than when I delegated it," says a business leader. This mature attitude releases organizational energy. It compels the delegating manager to grow and develop to more responsible jobs while it educates the subordinates to take over more and more of what the delegating manager has done. By educating his subordinates, the manager is educating himself. The old slogan that managers should make themselves unnecessary by making other people do what they have done has a very positive wisdom in it. But first and foremost, this is a way to develop the whole organization and its performance. This kind of delegation is doing well and is alive in many superior-subordinate relationships and in many companies. Unfortunately, opposite cases also exist.

Management is endowed with power, but not as exclusively as it is sometimes simplistically thought. In a present-day organization, no one is able to make decisions alone, even if she wanted to. In implementing decisions, many people need to be involved. Therefore, a manager must listen to many people before a decision can be made, and she has to gain the support of many people to get it implemented. All major decisions are processes; the end result of the process is the responsibility of the manager, and she needs power and authority to get it accepted by the many people concerned.

There is nothing shameful in power itself. Many good ideas have been left unrealized as the parent of the idea has had neither a powerful position nor the skill to influence. It is true that power has led to atrocities, but without it, good ideas cannot come true either. Power is not only a struggle for positions, but also a prerequisite of influence.

A manager can enlarge the responsibility of the people who report to him. But even then he maintains the responsibility that goes with his position including what he has delegated. Responsibility can be shared, but it cannot be divided. The "delegatees" are responsible to their superior the same way as the latter remains responsible to his own superior. In that sense, responsibility is undividable. In political power-play, it is important to secure one's position first and feel responsible for the outcome secondarily. In business, performance comes first. Whenever organizational politics takes precedence over performance, a deterioration in the morale and business is eventually seen.

In delegating and decentralizing, decisions are pushed to the lowest level where there are necessary resources for the decision. These resources exist often nearer to the operations than executives have had the chance to determine. Besides, the resources can be increased through decentralizing. This increases performance and makes the whole organization better. The power stays on the top, notwithstanding, but it is used to release energy and know-how and to authorize subordinates to make decisions. Even then, management must remain visible and expose itself to personal risks, so it can be credible and demand from others through the authority earned by its own performance. This is where management and leadership come together.

All managers have earned the promotion to a managerial position—in one way or another. During her career, a manager may have found it wise to centralize and keep power to herself for some time, at least. Sometimes promotions come as lucky strikes, sometimes as a result of a power struggle. Both cases may lead to problems later. In the first case, the manager may remain naive with regard to the power aspects of the organization; in the latter, she may become a victim of the ways by which she got the position. Of course, managers have developed and do develop from what they are when appointed managers. There are managers, it is true, who could be happier and better performing in nonmanagerial positions.

What about collective responsibility? Who is in charge in a collective responsibility—the collective body or its chairperson? In practice, this tends to remain ambiguous even when the responsibility is written in regulations. The boards of companies customarily consider the executive management responsible for the company and restrict themselves to the control function only; however, in associations, the issue is many times more complicated.

The manager (chairperson) of a collective body may find himself in a situation where he is expected, on behalf of the collectivity, to represent, stand, speak, and act for a decision that he, as a person, is not in favor of. An attempt can be made to talk over the predicament until a consensus is reached, but it does not always work out like that. If the conflict remains big enough and concerns an issue of strategic importance, it may be best for the manager to leave his position for someone who supports the majority view. At least this would be better than the kind of situation where the manager takes more effort to save his own skin than to ensure the performance of the organization. Government officials often encounter this predicament.

What about a manager who is more interested in promoting her own career than promoting the performance of her organization? This is like placing the cart before the horse. Credibility becomes an issue for anyone who considers her job just as a stepping stone to the next one. This kind of person is easily seen as an upstart, and she is not rewarded in the way she expects. In addition, this kind of person has not learned from any job really, as she has not gone through any educating difficulties nor received feedback from a long-term responsibility. Experiences from crises—company crises, career crises, personal crises—may be most educating as painful as they may temporarily feel (Darling, 1994).

MANAGERIAL ROLES

Roles are behavior patterns that belong to a position that the incumbent of the position is expected to play. Roles are characteristics of social positions, and role behaviors are shaped by the expectations of people to whom the position is of importance. Role theory is attributed to Sarbin and Allen (1968), but its roots can be traced at least to James, Binet, Dewey, and Durkheim in the nineteenth century. Bales and Slater, (1955), Katz and Kahn (1966), and Mintzberg (1973) have brought role theory to management research. In the following, the categorization of ten roles is adapted mainly from Mintzberg, who derived them initially from his observational study. This set of roles has had a very heuristic value in management education and training. The following exposition is influenced by feedback from managers whose work was analyzed using these ten roles (Nurmi, 1983).

The ten roles are divided into three groups: (1) interpersonal roles, (2) communicational roles, and (3) decisional roles. Mintzberg called his second group of roles informational, but in the material of Nurmi

(1983), the term communicational emerged as more adequate. In the following, these three groups are scrutinized.

Interpersonal Roles

A manager manages by managing other people. Management is often seen as managing subordinates to the extent that other important people are omitted. However, it is true that the superior-subordinate relationship is very central in management.

Every manager has his superior as well, and he is a link between his superior and his subordinates. In addition, the horizontal interpersonal relations with his colleagues in other departments influence his performance. Liaisons outside the company, and business and personal relations, may serve the managerial work as well. In all, a manager spends most of his time with other people influencing them and learning from them. Hence, interpersonal skills are necessary in any managerial job. But people seek to communicate with managers as well, due to the authority that the managerial position gives them. There are relationships that a manager cannot delegate, as it is only the managerial position that gives the prestige to the relationship that the other party may require.

There are three interpersonal roles: (1) figurehead, (2) superior, and (3) liaison. In Mintzberg's classification, the second role is the role of a leader (see Figure 4.1). The manager's role as a superior was proved eminent in the material of Nurmi (1987), and it is also quite important in management training. Leadership is the subject of Chapter 6 of this book, though in a meaning different from Mintzberg's. As Mintzberg himself points out, these kinds of delineations are somewhat arbitrary and must be judged in terms of their usefulness.

Figurehead

A manager is a symbol of her organization whenever she represents it in her job. Figurehead is the function of the position irrespective of the personal traits of job incumbent. The person can play the role better or worse depending on her traits, of course. Some people find representing to be stressing and straining; some may enjoy it. Nonetheless, neglecting this role means that even the

FIGURE 4.1. Interpersonal Roles

Interpersonal Roles	Description	Tasks
Figurehead	A personified figurehead, social and legal duties to represent the organization	Ceremonial tasks attached to position, giving addresses, honoring occasions by one's presence, mixer
Superior of the subordinates	Organizing, talking, listening, rewarding, controlling, delegating, motivating, requesting, commanding	All tasks related to subordinates
Liaison	Contacts and cooperation with other departments, organizations, or the public at large	Talks, meetings, correspondence, phone calls, etc.

Source: Adapted from Mintzberg (1973).

performance in other roles will not become visible enough. It is time-consuming, and it has optional costs. Honors are taken seriously only when received from a person in a managerial position. As a figure-head, a manager signs many papers where the value added by this action is negligible, and, yet, it is her signature that gives the paper its prestige. In the same way, a great many letters and other messages from outside the organization are addressed to the manager, as the sender hopes that his point will go to the manager of the organization. Usually the only thing that the manager can do is to behave as a figurehead, i.e., to delegate the issue to someone and sign the answer to the sender. Legal considerations require some issues to be decided by a high-level figurehead. Then, there are clients who refuse to deal with anyone but the senior manager. If answers to requests are signed by a manager, the client feels more assured that his point has received serious consideration. To be a figurehead includes representation and participation on important occasions, but also signing and dealing with routine and trifling matters.

Clearly, figurehead is an important and time-consuming role, and many managers feel that it takes too much time from the more down-to-earth, practical, and operational management. Yet, the neglect of this role jeopardizes the performance of the other roles because the role performance is measured by the influential others that the figurehead addresses. On the other hand, it is just one role among others. Some people may feel charmed to be a figurehead and feel themselves a very important person in dealing with trivia. Few organizations can afford a full-time figurehead, but they pay managers for performance, which presumes a greater value-added. A proper amount of being a figurehead is a necessary, but not sufficient, condition for managerial performance.

Superior

Being a superior is one of the most noticeable managerial roles. There are books galore that discuss this role, and it is a most popular subject in management training. It includes more or less formal tasks such as organizing the work of subordinates, division of work, and performance reviews. Meetings, job descriptions, reports, and organization charts among others belong to this more formal part of the role. But being in charge of the work of other people presupposes quite an amount of informal communication, interaction, listening, talking, encouraging, influencing, delegating, motivating, persuading, asking, and giving orders—well, the gamut of what interpersonal relations is.

As a superior, a manager is expected to correlate the objectives of the company and the objectives of her subordinates. There are company objectives that cannot be bargained with. However, there are good ideas, initiatives, and objectives of the subordinates that should be allowed to influence company objectives as well. The compatibility of the two is never perfect, though. A manager must be able to tolerate conflicts. Few organizations sound as harmonic symphonies do—most swing like jazz, with soloists, improvisers, and discordant beat.

Liaison

The role of the manager as a superior rests on formal, organizational authority. His horizontal relationships within and outside the organization do not have this backing. Yet, it is known that the horizontal liaison takes quite an amount of a manager's time. Observational studies seem to indicate that performance is correlated positively with the time consumed in liaison. Havas (1993) observed that new managers pay much attention to their new subordinates, while those who have been a longer time in a managerial job leave the organizational culture to the care of their subordinates and, instead, spend time in creating business in the liaison role.

Interpersonal skills are even more important in liaison than in the superior role, as there are no possibilities to manage by command in liaison. The need for liaisoning comes from the strategic necessity of all organizations, companies, units, and departments to fit with the environment, to adapt to it, and also to influence it. The environment is in a continuous flux; hence, liaisoning can never be finished. A manager is a transmitter of the outside into the inside and the inside into the outside of the organization. A manager is expected to create contacts and a network through which the fit of the organization and the environment can be enacted.

There are formal arrangements for managing the liaison role. Boards, committees, trade associations, and others may serve this function. Many unofficial meeting grounds such as clubs, associations, golf courses, gyms, etc. help liaisoning. But creating and opening channels requires always a personal, unofficial interaction—with or without the formal arrangements.

Communicational Roles

A manager is the center of the communication network in her organization. Often she may even be the bottleneck, as the information load is too heavy for her to absorb and interpret in terms of what to do with it. A manager receives more information than her subordinates. Nevertheless, she cannot stay at the mercy of the information, but she must be in active search for information, as the most important business information is seldom ready-made and documented. The information a manager receives and finds out is expected to be interpreted and communicated to others in an effort to influence and persuade them to act accordingly (Darling, 1991).

Despite the enormous information flow and sophisticated information technology, the most effective means of communication at a manager's disposal is personal interaction. Indeed, many excellent managers pay relatively little attention to reports and other written information. Instead, they talk and listen; they sense impressions and feelings; they rely on their personal judgment, even intuition (Mintzberg, 1973; Nurmi, 1983). Rumors and gossip have a story to tell (see Noon and Delbridge, 1993), even though they must be validated before decisive action is taken.

There are three communicational roles: (1) monitor, (2) informer, and (3) spokesman (Figure 4.2). In the following, each of them is described in detail.

Monitor

A manager receives and searches for information in its many forms for the purpose of decision making. Information and reporting systems serve this end; nonetheless, personal contacts remain the most potent means of learning what is going on. This is very true regarding what happens in the organization. Reports give only a partial version as compared to what a manager can sense by walking around (see Peters and Austin, 1985).

FIGURE 4.2. Communicational Roles

Communicational Roles	Description	Tasks
Monitor	Receives and searches information inside and outside organization, network center	Mail, discussion. phone calls, walking around
Informer	Informs and interprets information for the organization	Discussion, phone calls, notes, memos, letters, etc.
Spokesman	Speaks for the organization outside of it	Meetings, discussions, writing

Source: Adapted from Mintzberg (1973).

What happens outside the organization is even more difficult to learn by means of reports only. A manager needs to have an idea about the feelings and intentions of clients, competitors, subcontractors, markets at large, technological developments, political situations, etc. Some of this is communicated to him by his subordinates. Reports, the media, and correspondence cover one slice of it. A manager can get a report done for him about what he believes to be important before he makes any decisions. None of this can tell enough about the psychological and political atmosphere, which may be a most important factor for the decision making. Hence, nothing can replace sensing on the spot. "Management By Walking Around" (Peters and Austin, 1985) is a good managerial practice. Traveling, participating in conferences, going to exhibitions, meeting with clients, participating in clubs, even playing golf can give good hints about what is to be expected while documents are best in telling what has already happened.

The information that a manager receives from his different communication channels feeds his own decision making, but most of it he is expected to turn into action by interpreting and communicating it to someone else. This is why a manager may feel he is a bottleneck, as the information he receives may be too extensive for him to act upon under the continuous time pressure that he lives in.

Informer

One of the most frequent complaints that people level toward their superiors is that the superior does not give enough information. While there are managers who lack communication skills, it is also in the nature of managerial work that problems of communication are posed. It is easy to disseminate facts. But more often than not, the most important business and organizational information is not found in facts, but impressions, experiences, atmosphere, visions, and other kinds of soft information, which is much more difficult to share. In order to share this kind of "information," people need to share experiences in addition to words.

There are considerable cross-cultural communication differences that create problems in international communication. Japanese, Germans and Scandinavians may consider Anglo-Saxon small talk as a waste of time, while the latter may regard the former as blunt because of their lack of small talk. There is a voluminous amount of literature on cross-cultural communication (e.g., Kapoor, Hansén, and Davidson, 1991), which anyone working internationally should peruse. Nevertheless, a certain amount of confusion in cross-cultural communication is unavoidable.

Communication is a prerequisite for delegation. On delegating a responsibility to someone, the latter should have the resources that she needs in order to carry out the responsibility. One of the resources—and an easily forgotten one—is information. Some of this information cannot be transferred as it is based on the personal experience of the manager, and it cannot be shared with someone who has not had similar experiences. One reaction to this dilemma is to not delegate at all. But this is the worst choice; it leaves the manager with too many things to do, and as a consequence, she neglects her managerial duties and develops frustrated subordinates. Often, responsibilities must be delegated with the understanding that all information cannot be shared beforehand. This can be replaced by communication during and after delegation. This shared experience improves the communication on later occasions. The nature of managerial work implies communication and delegation problems. Understanding their nature, it is possible to live with them and—with patience—to improve communication and performance. It must be born in mind that very often when someone does not do what a manager expected, this is due to communication failure inherent in delegating rather than a failure in the responsibility as such.

Spokesman

People outside the organization take communication more seriously if it is communicated by someone from managerial echelons. Particularly in crises, management is expected to stand out and speak for the organization (Darling, 1994). The media has grown more and more influential in public opinion; hence, managers have had to learn to communicate the media. In addition, personal rapport and communication with influential constituents of the organization is a part of managerial work. So, a manager's manager had better learn news first from his subordinate than from someone else. The board requires a special treatment in communication from the executives. Very important persons (VIPs) outside the organization include clients (including clients in the same company), subcontractors, trade unions, civil servants of importance, local and national politicians, etc. Many times a manager is also an expert in his field, and he may be asked to give speeches or advice and be a member on committees and task forces. All this may provide an opportunity to be a spokesman for the organization as well.

Turning the information into action is more difficult outside the organization than inside it. A spokesman's role consequently requires even more communication skills than an informer's role. Spokesmanship is growing in importance in an era that has been characterized as the information society (e.g., Toffler, 1990), in which media can make or break phenomena and borderlines of companies become fluid in their networks with other companies and other economic agents.

Decisional Roles

Decisions are results of managerial work. Managers are paid for making decisions. Everybody likes to make nice decisions, but managers are expected to make risky, tough, unpleasant, unpopular, and painful decisions as well. Inability to make decisions is an unforgivable sin for a manager. In fact, even many erroneous but timely decisions are not as bad, as they can be corrected later. However, a decision that was not made when it was necessary often results in lost opportunity. A manager remains personally responsible for the decisions even if he relied on others to make them. One decision detrimental enough to the organization may get a manager fired. There are four decisional roles: (1) entrepreneur, (2) disturbance handler, (3) resource allocator, and (4) negotiator (Figure 4.3).

Entrepreneur

A manager is not expected only to manage things as they occur, but she is expected to be an initiator, developer, and innovator, a person who makes things happen instead of letting them happen or reacting to them when they happen. In this respect, every manager is an entrepreneur; she may not have monetary investments in her organization, but a manager is expected to have a vested, intrinsic interest in what she is doing.

In her interpersonal and communicational roles, a manager learns about opportunities in the environment and strengths of her orga-

FIGURE 4.3. Decisional Roles

Decisional Roles	Description	Tasks
Entrepreneur	Seizes opportunities, initiates and controls development projects	Ideation, strategy formation, control, project management
Disturbance handler	Managing unexpected, urgent emergencies	Discussions, arbitration, grievance handling, commands, reprimands, control
Resource allocator	Allocation of men, money, material, and time. Deciding or confirming strategic issues of the organization	Planning, programming, authorizing, deciding
Negotiator	Representing the organization on important issues	Negotiating

Source: Adapted from Mintzberg (1973).

nization. In her role as an entrepreneur, she utilizes all this and creates and seizes new business ideas and opportunities. In the same way, she learns about threats and weaknesses and can circumvent them early—before they harm the company.

New opportunities emerge all the time. Some are being launched; some are being prepared; some take the form of a project; some are shelved; some are rejected; some are finalized; some are implemented. It is not enough for a manager that he is innovative; he must, in addition, fuel his people with creativity and entrepreneurship. Pinchot (1985) calls this intrapreneurship in distinction from entrepreneurship based on ownership. Managers as intrapreneurs must be personally involved in development projects to add to their own credibility.

In the role of an entrepreneur, a manager can never be quite satisfied with the way things are. There are always ways to improve performance, and someone will sooner or later do it in this or some other organization. Indeed, it seems as if it would be possible to predict the performance of an organization by the distribution of satisfaction in it. When the management feels worried, but operating people are satisfied, the outlook of future performance is positive; but when the management is happy, and the operative people feel worried, the outlook is often gloomier.

Disturbance Handler

As an entrepreneur, a manager causes things to happen. As a disturbance handler, he reacts to things that he did not initiate, want, nor even expect to happen. Major disturbances call for urgent action notwithstanding. They arise from sudden environmental surprises, unforeseen consequences of entrepreneurial action, long-nourished crises that come out in the open all of a sudden, and neglected problems, etc. Fires, industrial action, the resigning of a key person (particularly, if he is joining a competitor), the loss of an important client (particularly, if he goes to a competitor), a big enough mistake, and the conflict between subordinates are examples of disturbances that demand quick managerial action.

It is difficult to plan disturbance handling. When emergencies occur, they take priority and tend to affect all schedules. Even if the disturbance cannot be solved quickly, usually a "truce" is attempted to allow time to cool down and appease the situation. Managers are allowed or even expected to be tougher and even autocratic in crises as Hamblin demonstrated as early as in 1958. There is no time for consulting nor democratic decision making if the house is on fire. The credibility of a manager is being tested in a crisis, and he may earn a heroic or a cowardly reputation depending on his crisis management skills (Darling, 1994).

Disturbances are in the nature of managerial work, and they tend to increase in a time of great and abrupt transformations. Neither the world nor its organizations can be planned strictly enough to avoid surprises and disturbancies. While laymen may see managerial work as a lucrative, prestigious, high-and-mighty position, disturbance handling is one of its unpleasant dimensions.

Resource Allocator

A manager is in charge of the resources allocated to her and on their further allocation, utilization, and return. The three Ms—men, money, and material—are usually listed among resources. Know-how, technology, time, and image can be added to the list. All decision making is resource bound; it is limited by available resources, and it concerns their allocation and augmentation.

There are methods and systems for the allocation of resources. Organization charts, production plans, work schedules, project plans, etc., allocate people. Men, money, and material are allocated by means of budgeting. However, budgeting or other systems and methods do not decide anything. There are not only accounting processes, but also political processes involved. The budgeting game occurs in many organizations (Hofstede, 1967; Lumijärvi, 1990). The subordinates ask more resources for less return on the resources while their superiors are willing to allocate less resources and insist more for their return. Likewise, an organization chart does not make people work together. The formal procedures are an aid to a manager's decision making, but it is her own judgment that is the most critical and irreplaceable decision support of all.

Time is the most limited of resources. Yet, so many projects, people, meetings, deadlines, intentions, and disturbances—the list knows no limits—compete intensely for a manager's time. There are modern time-planning systems and methods, but again, they do not set priorities; they do not replace the will and perseverance of a manager to find time for what is important nor do they say "no" to what is not important. A manager does not only manage his own time, but his priorities extend throughout his organization. The mismanagement of time leads to quite an amount of waste.

There is vast literature on quantitative methods in decision making and resource allocation. Modern information technology has made their use easy enough for anyone. Still, they have been of limited use. It just seems that managers prefer to use their minds, the mental models that have been developed and shaped by their personal experiential learning. These models contain information and decision aids that are hard to write down in a simple formula, but they are more flexible and pertinent to variable managerial situations than any computed model can be. Naturally, they can lead to mistakes and to drastic ones at that. This is the risk that anyone in a managerial position must bear. If the mistake is big enough, the manager's job is at stake.

Negotiator

Managerial work is talking, listening, influencing, being influenced—in brief, negotiating. According to casual inquiries in management courses, some managers spend more than 20 percent of the working time in negotiating, and the number of managers who spend a great deal of time negotiating is considerable. Managerial work requires negotiating skills.

The negotiator role is discernable from the other roles even less clearly than the others are from each other. The role appears practically always in connection with, and at the same time as, one or more of the other roles. So figurehead, spokesman, and resource allocator are always also a negotiator. It is not uncommon that negotiations are interrupted to get someone prestigious enough on spot to accept, confirm, or ratify what has been agreed upon in the talks so far. This shows that the negotiator role is attached to a managerial position.

The PCD Model of Managerial Work

Managerial work was illustrated with Mintzberg's set of ten roles. Without a simplification like this, it would be impossible to describe the complexity, diversity, and ambiguity of managerial work. In practice, the roles are not easily discernable, but they are entwined in many intricate ways. A manager is always playing many roles simultaneously. A manager can at the same time be a superior, a monitor, an informer, an entrepreneur, and a negotiator. The roles comprise a whole, and each of them can be understood only in the context of the whole set.

Figure 4.4 reduces the managerial work to a PCD model, with the acronym derived from Persons, Communication, and Decisions. The most important information comes from persons by way of communicating, and it is processed into decisions; however, a manager can carry out the decisions only with the help of other persons.

FIGURE 4.4. PCD Model of Management

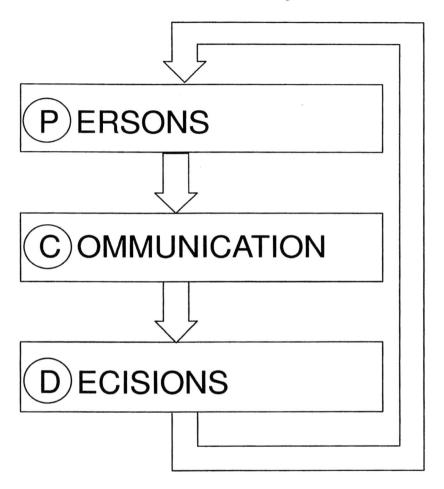

Source: Adapted from Mintzberg (1973).

It is a consequence of this entwinement of roles that a manager cannot specialize on a few roles only, even if he feels more comfortable in some roles than in others. Different situations call for different roles disregarding the preferences of the manager. In different managerial positions, the roles have differing importance. So in marketing, interpersonal roles have more weight than the other roles, whereas for managers of staff departments, the communicational roles are prominent. A manager is, however, a generalist. So, the smartest person of a company without adequate interpersonal skills cannot be but a poor manager, as he cannot implement his smart ideas without the help of others. Likewise, a nice person in interpersonal relations with an inability to decide is in a managerial position suffocating his organization. A manager need not be perfect—these kinds of people are in very short supply. A manager does need to be satisfactorily good in a wide set of roles instead of being fantastic in one or two of them.

REVIEW QUESTIONS

1. Describe the evolution of the management concept.

2. Describe the relationship between the existence of power and the activity of delegation.

3. What are the various interpersonal roles of management? Discuss.

4. What are the various communication roles of management? Discuss.

5. What are the various decisional roles of management? Discuss.

LEARNING EXERCISES

1. How do persons, communications, and decisions define managerial roles in your company?

2. How do the various management role types balance out in your own management position?

3. Analyze your own strengths and weaknesses with regard to each of the management role types.

4. How do you plan to improve your performance in the various role types needed in your management position?

Chapter 5

Managerial Work

Happy are those who dream dreams, and are ready to pay the price to make them come true.

—Cardinal Suenens

ORGANIZING

Organizing is, along with planning, coordinating, and delegating, among the most classic of management functions in management literature (e.g., Megginson, Mosley, and Pietri, 1992, pp. 19-22). It is, however, also a most practical job of a manager to organize things, people, jobs, projects, responsibilities, departments, and units. Organizing, in this sense, means structuring the joint work of people in a way that the objectives of the organization are reached (see Darling and Nurmi, 1995).

Groups of people can be organized, or they organize themselves horizontally and vertically (Figure 5.1). In the horizontal division of labor, people specialize in functions, departments, units—the functional division among manufacturing, marketing, product development, etc., is a typical horizontal specialization. The vertical division is between managerial and operative work. There is a trend and a necessity to make the borderlines and specializations much less rigid and much more fluid, permeable, and even interchangeable than in the mechanical organization thinking (see, e.g., Snow, Miles, and Coleman, 1992). This does not mean chaos, however. Even though the structures are less permanent, it remains for a manager to think which are the key functions in her area of responsibility and how to organize the division and cooperation of the functions. The following

FIGURE 5.1. Horizontal and Vertical Division of Labor

Vertical division of labor

	Management
Task, functional,	departmental, and federal divisions
	Operations

Horizontal division of labor

basic structural alternatives are presented in both small and large organizations.

Companies very often get started by one person, the founder. As his amount of work increases and exceeds his capacity to do it all by himself, he employs people around him. But he may like to exert control by himself. The organization is a one-man show (Figure 5.2). Everything leads to this one person.

In a one-man show, the one and only manager keeps everything or at least as much as he can to himself. He gives the others tasks one at a time as if they are just doing errands. This kind of an organization is almost the normal one in the early phases of an entrepreneur. He knows the products best; he may even be their designer and manufacturer. He may even know all his customers in person, and thus he may find it difficult to allow anyone elseto work with his customers. In a

FIGURE 5.2. One-Man Show

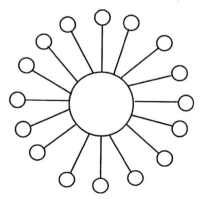

small company, the one-man show may perform excellently, and even the subordinates may like to work for an entrepreneur who can decide quickly and respond personally. But with growth, one person cannot manage all of it forever. The need for change in organization and management style becomes urgent sooner or later, but the company is in many cases as much of a love affair as a business to its founder. Giving up some of his control and authority may be very painful or downright impossible for him. His personal crisis is at the same time an organizational crisis. The saving of the company may require new management.

Functional division of labor is basic in organizational thinking. Even though modern organizational thinking emphasizes the flow between the functions rather than their specialization, there are basic functions that each and every organization must take care of. All organizations have a product (service) that is produced and marketed, and the markets, in turn, create demand for products (Figure 5.3). Management and administration direct this process and flow between functions.

Companies are founded and established based on a product. Too often they even die around the same product, as they have neglected product development, and competitors have made the old product

FIGURE 5.3. Functional Organization

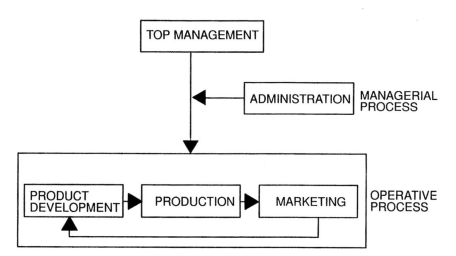

obsolete. This has happened even for big companies—Morris-Mini and Xerox copiers are classic examples of excellent products for which strong competitors entered the market. The product development (or even research and development) function is needed in all companies, even if it may not be organized as a department.

The production consists of manufacturing and its services. In industry, a major share of the resources of a company is involved in production; production is where cost leadership is often won or lost.

When competition has intensified in most businesses, marketing has become the key function. It sells present products and picks ideas from the market for product development. The latter feedback seldom works as well as it could.

Even though product development, production, and marketing exist in one way or another in all companies—indeed, in all organized endeavors—they need not be departmentalized. In the knowledge business, the developer or inventor of a product may be its best producer and salesperson, as she is the expert and the enthusiast to tell about its benefits. Business processes based on the value chain (Porter, 1985) organize the chains or flows of activities from the order of the customer to the delivery of the product. This organizing principle builds on horizontal flow and cross-functional management rather than on departmentalization (Harrington, 1991; Ascari, Rock, and Dutta, 1995). It has been applied successfully in Asea Brown Bovery, a major European manufacturer of transportation equipment, as well as in other companies.

A company is not required to have all functions that it needs to have its own governance. Functions can be bought from the market so that a company can focus on its own core competence. A company may, for instance, subcontract the whole production, and only specialize on marketing (as marketing companies do). This kind of interorganizational organizing (Grandori and Soda, 1995) has increased to the extent that the term "networking" has become popular to describe the whole of economy. Transaction-cost analysis (Williamson, 1991) renders conceptual instruments to analyze which functions would be better inside the company, i.e., governed by hierarchy, and which would be better bought outside, i.e., governed by the market. Lehtimäki, Kontkanen and Nurmi (1991) have applied this approach to knowledge-intensive organizations.

When the organization grows further, federal units (profit centers, strategic business units) dealing with products, branches, types of clients, or geographical areas are organized (Figure 5.4). Now, the functions are organized within the units. Profit centers can be grouped into divisions that are governed by headquarters of an individual firm or a holding company (see Campbell, Goold, and Alexander, 1995) (Figures 5.5, 5.6, and 5.7).

Matrix structures crossbreed products, business units, geographical areas, staff departments, service functions, and projects into two- or more dimensional structural networks (Figures 5.8 and 5.9). While they are more adequate descriptions of the organizational reality, they run the risk of losing the core concern and the focus of the business. Complex forms may begin to live a life of their own, but it is true as well that the organization of big, diversified, international corporations is so complex that no organization chart can provide an adequate description. These complex organizational structures do not belong to the organizing function of daily managerial work. Building them up and reshuffling them takes a deliberate effort and is a project that must be managed from the very top of the organization.

MANAGEMENT BY OBJECTIVES

Management by objectives has a long history. However, it is fair to credit Peter Drucker in his writings in the 1950s for promoting

FIGURE 5.4. Profit-Center Organization

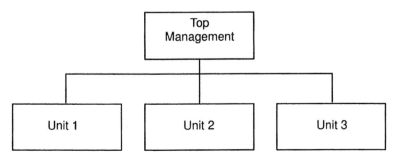

FIGURE 5.5. Divisional Organization

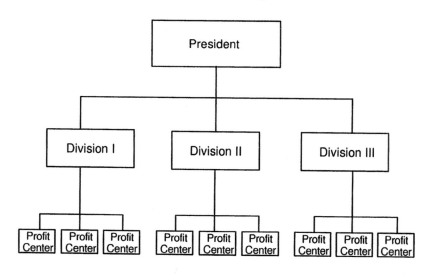

FIGURE 5.6. A Conglomerate

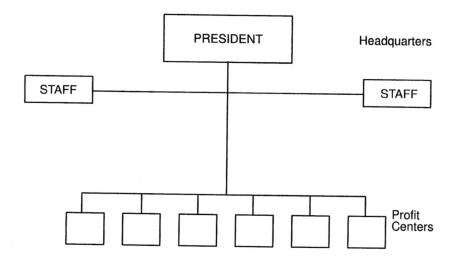

the idea of management by objectives as a philosophy. In essence, management by objectives (MBO*) means:

1. A company, its units, departments, and people should be managed by objectives instead of individual tasks.
2. Objectives are set in superior-subordinate communications throughout the organization.
3. Performance is reviewed against the objectives.
4. The review of deviations from objectives is a learning exercise and fosters a more realistic setting of objectives and performance for the next period.

Later these basic principles of Drucker have been elaborated, and techniques, forms, methods, procedures, policies, and systems have been introduced for the setting of objectives, for superior-subordinate communications, and for other phases of the management process. Many variations and many names have been introduced (e.g., Humble, 1968; Odiorne, Weinrich, and Mendleson, 1980; Santalainen and Hunt, 1988), but they share, by and large, the four preceding points. In some variations, the principles have been lost in too sophisticated techniques or in bureaucracy. In some applications, particularly in public administration, quantitative output is measured in absolute terms and on a short time-span without setting objectives. This has led to macabre consequences (see Zilbert, 1991): the organization is being directed toward what can be measured in numbers instead of toward its mission. Yet, the number of extinguished fires may not be an adequate measure of a fire brigade's performance even though it is easier to measure than the preventive work against fires. The point in setting objectives is for people to learn to see what is essential in their job in the future. On the other hand, measuring output without objectives focuses on what is past and gone. It is as bizarre a way of directing the future as it would be driving a car looking at the rear mirror only.

Figure 5.10 illustrates the basic elements of management by objectives. The first is the job; it must be designed to allow the job incumbent to plan, do, and control his job. Job descriptions are used

---

*MBO has later come to stand for Management Buy Out as well. The two usages of the acronym have created confusion at times.

FIGURE 5.7. A Specimen of a Diversified International Corporation

NESTE CORPORATION'S OPERATION STRUCTURE
AS OF JANUARY 1, 1992

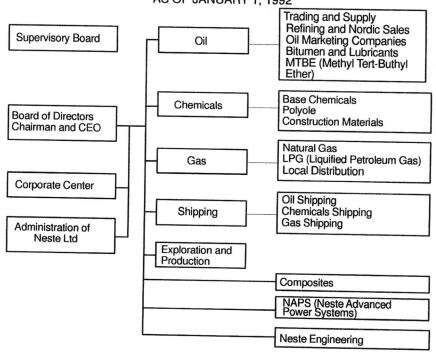

commonly to link the job incumbent and the organization. Some companies have used detailed lists of tasks for the purpose, but they have proved to be cumbersome and change-resistant to the extent that many companies have ceased to do any job descriptions at all as the jobs may change more rapidly than any detailed list of tasks can follow. Therefore, instead of trying to list the inputs to a job, it may be better to delineate the responsibilities, objectives, and expected outputs on a general level. What tasks do they include and how they are carried out remains for the responsible person to decide as long as he is working toward his objectives.

The process of formulating job descriptions is in actual practice more important than their form. There are companies in which job

FIGURE 5.8. The Matrix of Production and Service

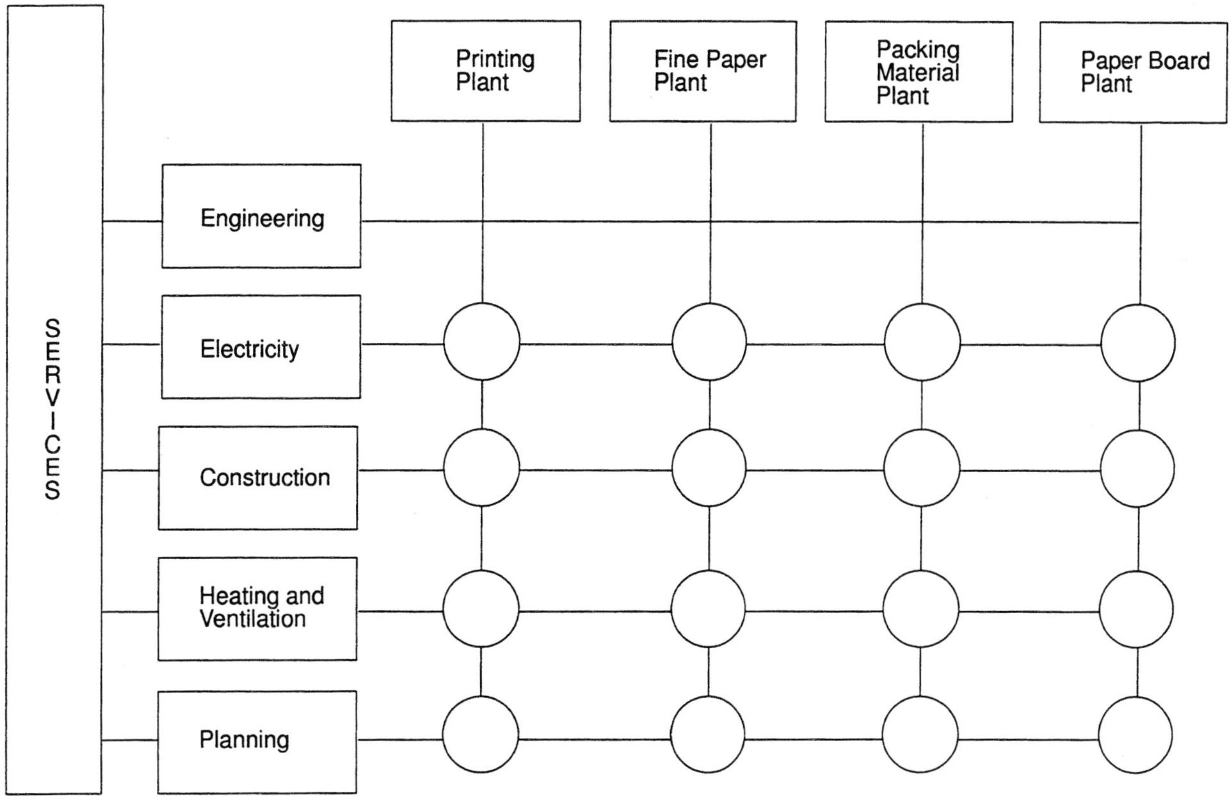

FIGURE 5.9. A Matrix of Functions and Development Projects

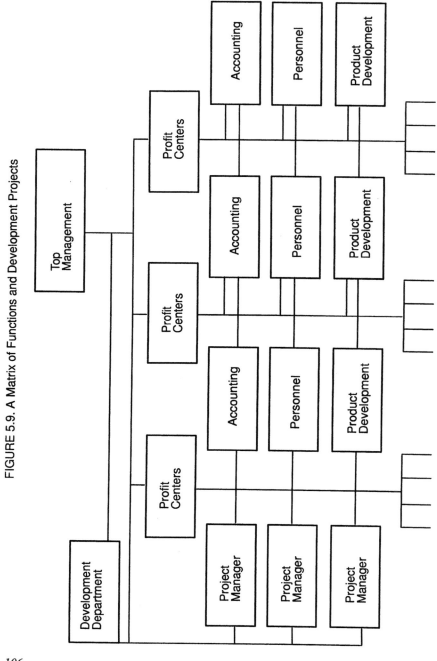

descriptions are written by a staff department. Some superiors like to write them for their subordinates. This way of compiling them is likely to have little impact. At best, the job description is an *agreement* between a superior and a subordinate; it may be written on paper. The communication and agreement are primary; the form of the document is secondary. There are many good forms of job descriptions. One that works in a company is in Figure 5.11.

In the example, the responsibilities are listed in six points:

1. The contents of the responsibility, i.e., the primary and secondary functions
2. Economic responsibility (which in the instance of managing director is accountability on profitability—financing is mentioned in addition; in production, economic responsibility is usually accountability on costs)
3. Administrative responsibility
4. Technical or expert responsibility; not mentioned in the example in Figure 5.10—is most important in staff positions, but also in research and development, marketing (knowledge of markets, products, and marketing) and production (production and product technology)
5. Responsibility for development
6. Responsibility for the strategy

The latter two are combined into the example of Figure 5.10, but in many jobs they are differentiated. Key result areas are likewise listed in the example, but they may be on a different form as well. Forms and applications may vary, but it is crucial that jobs are organized as responsibilities instead of a collection of tasks for management by objectives to be applied in an appropriate way.

The responsibility is incarnated in the job incumbent as a person. Every manager must know the people who work for him by way of personal communication and joint work better than any professional consultant can do. There is, of course, lots of daily, casual communication. In addition, regular reviews of objectives, performance, work improvement plans, and individual development plans have proved to be useful.

Objectives (Figure 5.10) are set in communication between each superior-subordinate pair. This particular communication is called performance review. This communication is the crux of the whole process, and it makes management by objectives a dynamic exercise or a piece of deadwood. On agreeing about the objectives, the responsible person has brought authority to act in line with the objectives during the period that the objectives hold. It is up to him to decide what to do, how to do it, and when to do it. Only he works toward the objectives. In case of something that jeopardizes the objectives, he had better inform his superior. Otherwise, the superior is left with the contention that everything goes as agreed in setting the objectives.

For people to be able to plan their work and to get feedback from it, a proper information system is needed. It should first and foremost feed the person in charge with information. The reports may confirm

FIGURE 5.10. Elements of Management by Objectives

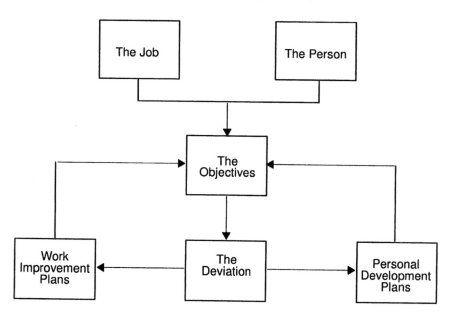

FIGURE 5.11. A Description of Job Responsibilities

DESCRIPTION OF A RESPONSIBILITY AREA

Job: Managing Director

Superior: The Chairman of the Board

Subordinates:

Administrative Manager
Production Manager
Marketing Manager
Project Manager

I.   **Description of the Job**

A. Managing director is in charge of the company and its long-term profitability

B. More specifically
   1. The managing director is in charge of the whole company including:
      • Administration
      • Production
      • Marketing
      • Development projects
   2. The profitability of the company
   3. The financing of the company
   4. The one-year planning of the company including:
      • Budgeting principles
      • The budget and its implementation
   5. The management of the company including:
      • The principles and system of management
      • The framework of goal setting of the company
      • The agreement of the objectives of his direct subordinates in the responsibility area
      • The control of the implementation of the objectives
   6. The strategy and development of the company including:
      • Strategies of the company
      • The product-market mix of the company
      • The goal setting of the development work of the company

II. **Output Areas**

A. Return on investment
B. Turnover by products and customer segments
C. Growth percent by products
D. Liquidity
E. The objectives of personnel development
F. Pollution reduction down to the norms

FIGURE 5.11 (continued)

III.   Limits of authority

A. Decisions to be submitted to the board
1. The confirmation of the strategy of the company
2. The confirmation of the one-year objectives
3. Legal considerations

B. To inform to the board
1. Deviations from confirmed objectives
2. Matters affecting the public image of the company

IV.   Liaison functions

A. Representative of the company
B. Secretary of the board of the company
C. In charge of the cooperation of direct subordinates (head of management committee)
D. In charge of development projects in liaison with the managers of production, marketing, and projects (the meeting of the development group)

TOP MANAGEMENT

- Profitability, return on investment
- Sales or respective figure of volume in monetary terms
- Market share
- Company image
- Management development objectives
- Strategic objectives
- Financial objectives

MARKETING

- Sales volume
- Contribution to the margin of sales
- Pricing
- Market share
- Customer distribution
- Sales by products
- Product image
- Order size
- Sales outlets
- The turnover of inventory
- The number of returns

PRODUCTION

- Production volume
- Production costs
- Delivery time
- Product quality
- Turnover of personnel
- Accidents
- Absenteeism
- Rejects
- Waste of material

RESEARCH AND DEVELOPMENT

- New products
- Product quality
- Technical expertise
- The competence of personnel
- Objectives for the development of existing products
- Objectives for new ideas
- Meeting the development deadlines
- Project objectives

ADMINISTRATION

- Deadlines of reports
- Deadlines of the collection of credits due to costs of administration
- Objectives of installing administrative methods
- Costs of interest
- Turnover of financing property
- The amount of lost cash discounts

PURCHASES AND PROCUREMENT

- Purchasing prices
- Times of delivery
- Turnover of inventory
- The interests of stock property
- Indirect costs of procurement
- Optimal level of inventory
- The amount of purchases

FIGURE 5.11 (continued)

PERSONNEL
- Internal image of the company
- The turnover of personnel
- Absenteeism
- Accidents
- Personnel costs
- The amount of personnel
- The competence of personnel
- Objectives of personnel recruitment
- Return on investment per capita
- Objectives of induction program
- Objectives of training and development programs

MAINTENANCE DISTURBANCES
- Breaks and interruptions of production
- Costs of maintenance
- Production standards and the like

KNOWLEDGE WORKERS
- Objectives for the acquisition of new knowledge
- Objectives for the distribution of knowledge
- Objectives for the impact of knowledge
- Project objectives
- Deadlines

THE MANAGEMENT OF AN EMPLOYMENT OFFICE
- The amount of unemployment
- Objectives for the mobility of labor
- Objectives of training programs
- To get a forecast of labor force conducted
- Deadlines

A MANAGER OF ROAD CONSTRUCTION
- The cost of construction
- The cost, amount, and deadlines of projects
- Fluctuation of the amount of workers
- Work safety
- Safety of the roads

TEACHER
- The percent of students who get the degree
- The competence of students
- The employment of students
- Objectives for the contents of the studies
- Objectives for the development training methods

that things go as planned. In case a deviation appears, corrective measures must be developed. This belongs to the superior as well, as the deviation may cause a change in his plans, too. But in a good information system, it is the responsible person who is the first to know, and it is up to him to go and talk about it to his superior if he finds that the deviation will affect objectives.

Deviations are the rule rather than the exception. This need not mean that things have been managed badly. The objectives may have been unrealistic, or something unforeseen may have happened. Nonetheless, it is the open review and communication of deviations that teach realistic setting of objectives for the next period and also help to make the unforeseen visible. Setting objectives is learned by setting objectives and analyzing the deviations. In this analysis, the bottlenecks of the operations are revealed, the essential from the unessential discerned, and feedback from what has been done received. The analysis of deviations is an excellent instrument for learning on the job.

Any statement about how things should be done does not work as an objective. Objectives are set to steer the action toward an intended direction and degree. For the purpose, they must be concrete, specific, realistic, and challenging enough. Too many objectives are a symptom that the essence of the job has not been understood. It may be advisable to think first about the key result areas of the job and then to think what kind of objectives can be set for each. An objective should be measurable. "to improve profitability" is not concrete and measurable enough to steer action, whereas "to improve profitability by so much" is.

On the other hand, measurability should not take priority over the mission and the key result areas. The measure need not and should not be more accurate than the phenomenon it measures. Crude and qualitative objectives are quite useful for the steering purpose. For instance, the number of new products as an objective in product development is admittedly crude, but even as such, if the agreed number is not reached, the analysis of the deviation is likely to provide illuminating suggestions. Product quality, competence of personnel, and the quality of service are examples of areas in which qualitative objectives can be set. If there appears to be a job where no objectives can be set, it may be an indication that the job is not needed at all. The point in setting objectives is to search for key result areas, not the precision of measurement as such. No numbers can ever replace human judgment.

The setting of objectives is specific to a company, specific to a job, specific to a situation. It does not work by copying. Figure 5.11 gives examples in some jobs, and they may trigger an analysis of a particular job in a particular company at a particular time.

It is a basic idea in management by objectives that when each individual works toward her objectives she works toward the company objectives. This means that the objectives of different persons must be somehow coordinated vertically and horizontally in an organization. It helps if marketing sells what production manufactures. The person in charge knows best her responsibility, and she should set the objectives for her job. But one of the functions of performance reviews is to make the individual objectives meet with the company objectives. The company objectives are expressed by the top management in its expectations for the period, but horizontal communication and teamwork also facilitate the process. In this process, the operative objectives in management by objectives come to interact with strategic objectives. The more open the communication in the company, the less time this all takes—if the communication is not working, the resulting bureaucracy is time consuming and slows down everything (Darling, 1991).

As a performance review is so important a communication, the superior and subordinate should prepare themselves to do it properly. The superior must make her objectives clear to her subordinate.* The subordinate is in the best position to analyze the deviations in his job during the past period and set objectives for the next period. From these grounds, the most important part of the review—the objectives for the next period—can be discussed and agreed upon. The past is for learning, instead of blaming or defending, while the future lies ahead to be influenced by means of realistic objectives.

What is agreed in the review can be jotted down on a form—a specimen form is presented in Figure 5.12. Once again, the commu-

---

*Actually, the terms "superior" and "subordinate" are misleading as management by objectives releases both from control from the above. Both have responsibilities of their own that are coordinated in the review. Terms such as "persons in charge" or "responsible persons" would be better fitting, but they are clumsy to use repeatedly in the text, so the traditional shorter, though inadequate terms are used.

FIGURE 5.12. A Form for Performance Review

OUTPUT	PERIOD 1				PERIOD 2	
	Objec-tive	Re-sult	Devi-ation	What to do?	Objec-tive	Re-sult
SALES	a $	b $	c $	Does not work via an agent; own sales organization needed	d $	
RECLA-MATION	a at most	b	c	Insufficient service; training necessary	a at most	

nication is more important than the form. It is known that some superiors dictate the objectives on the form. There are, however, few superbosses who could know everything better than their subordinates. Dictation does not lead to commitment either. This danger always lurks around the corner even if the superior does not want it to, as even the subordinates may be badly prepared for the review or, for one reason or another, do not have enough initiative of their own. On the other hand, management by objectives is a means to add and seize the initiative that people naturally have although it is much too often blocked by the organization.

The analysis of deviation in the performance review gives rise to two kinds of development plans: (1) the work improvement plan and (2) the individual development plan.

Work improvement plans can be written down like the one in Figure 5.13. They are easiest to manage as projects, which have objectives regarding quantity, quality, costs, and deadlines. The resources for development projects are always limited. Therefore,

FIGURE 5.13. A Form for Work Improvement Plans

PROBLEM	OBJECTIVE	IN CHARGE	DEADLINE	IMMEDIATE ACTION
The estab-lishing of a sales organization in Sweden	A sales or-ganization established in Sweden selling Y dollars	Marketing manager	1/1/199x	A detailed plan till 1/1/199x
Service training etc.	The reduc-tion of reclam-ations to not more than A a year	Sales manager	1/12/199x	Discuss with personnel manager to get the schedule till 1/2/199x

their priorities must be assessed in accordance with their contribution to the company performance. What cannot be implemented in this period can be reassessed and reconsidered for the next period.

The individual development plan, when derived from the performance review, links training and education of people to the development of their work. The two do not always meet in company practice. The development plan, again, is a matter of communication with the two responsible persons, and it requires openness and communication skills from both parties. This is facilitated by adequate preparation. Figure 5.14 exemplifies points in the preparation. Figure 5.15 is a trigger for the communication in the discussion itself—the discussion is by no means limited to the points raised in it, and, naturally, any relevant issue can be raised. The discussion is confidential, but its outcome in a general form can be reported to the manager on the next level, as he may have a better chance to act upon the issues on hand. In addition, facts can be sent to the personnel department as input for their training plans.

FIGURE 5.14. A Form to Prepare for the Potential Review

POTENTIAL REVIEW

*Name:*_____

*Job:*_____

1. Are you by and large interested in your present job?

   _____
   _____
   _____

2. What about it would you like to be changed?

   _____
   _____
   _____

3. Where do you need support, guidance, and/or training to be able to do your job in the future?

   _____
   _____
   _____
   _____
   _____

4. What action do you suggest for the next year?

   _____
   _____
   _____
   _____
   _____

Superior:_____

Person in charge:_____

Seen superior:_____

FIGURE 5.15. A Specimen Form to Use in Preparing for the Potential Review

It is a policy in our company that each superior and his subordinate review in October how we can best help people to develop in their work, increase satisfaction in the work, and prepare for future challenges.

The main purpose of the review is to help you. It is important that you prepare yourself for it so that you can benefit from it. In this form, some questions are presented to you for the purpose of helping your preparation. It is not mandatory to fill out this form. You need not limit yourself to issues raised in this form. It is meant to trigger your own thinking.

You can discuss anything relevant in the review. Its usefulness for you depends on your contribution to it. You are supposed to write down what you agreed on objectives and directions of development. Your superior is prepared to discuss with you any suggestions that you have about your job and your future. He gives his views about them knowing practical possibilities and his possibilities to help you. He presents some of his views for your ears only in order to help you. Note that you need not discuss anything private or anything else that you do not wish to discuss.

1. What do you think are the most important tasks in your present job?

_____
_____
_____
_____

2. Which of them take the most of your time, care, and attention?

_____
_____
_____
_____

3. Do you find that you can use your capabilities, education, experience, and interests in your present job? If not, which would you like to use more? How could we change your job to make this possible?

_____
_____
_____
_____

4. Think of your achievements in your present job. What kind of difficulties have you experienced?

_____
_____
_____
_____

5. Is there something unnecessary or meaningless in your job? What?

_____
_____
_____
_____

6. What kind of work would interest you in the future? Probably many alternatives come to your mind. Would they require specific experience or training? If they do, how do you plan to acquire this experience or training?

_____
_____
_____
_____

7. Is there anything in your job that you are dissatisfied with or need information about? Do you have any suggestions to make the company a better place to work?

_____
_____
_____
_____

8. What do you expect this year from

- yourself?
- your superior?
- the management of the company?
- your subordinates?
- someone else?

_____
_____
_____
_____

THE SUPERIOR-SUBORDINATE RELATIONSHIP

Delegating

Organization is not a chart on a paper. Organization is working together, living together; organization is interaction. There is no structure that would release managers from managing. The horizontal division of labor between a manager and those who report to him is not a matter of job description and objectives as they stand on paper—it is, first of all, a matter of delegating. It presumes delegation skills from the superior and ability and willingness to accept responsibility from the one delegated to.

The superior-subordinate relationship is a quintessence of management, and along with it, the structural and systemic frames of an organization become alive or stagnate. It is not just a work relationship, but its effects tend to spill over into the life outside the working hours. In the following, this relationship is viewed, on the one hand, as a matter of top-to-bottom delegation and, on the other hand, as a matter of taking charge, being held accountable, and even managing from bottom to top. The two aspects are interdependent. If they support each other, they add to the integrity of all concerned. If the two are in conflict, the trouble will not be restricted to the two parties only.

Delegating is handing down authority, responsibility, and decision making to a subordinate level in the framework of agreed upon objectives. It is a lot more than assigning a task to be performed. Delegation includes planning, doing, choice of the way of doing, and even control from a manager to his subordinate.

Is it possible to delegate responsibility? This is a matter of disagreement in the literature (see McFarland, 1974, pp. 366-379). The subordinates are accountable for their performance to their superior. In management by objectives, the attaining of objectives counts for performance. Then a superior can delegate, in the same way, responsibility to his subordinate, meaning that the subordinate is responsible to him. But it is as essential that the superior in question is responsible to his own superior for what he has delegated. He cannot escape from responsibility by giving it up to his subordinates. Responsibility can be shared, but it cannot be delegated. In that sense, the maxim of the undivisibility of responsibility holds good. However, this is not an adequate excuse for centralizing power and authority to one person only.

This discussion implies another paradox of delegation. Whenever the subordinate succeeds in what has been delegated to him, he earns the credit for it—including his superior's thanks and appreciation; if the subordinate fails in what has been delegated to him, the superior has failed in his delegation, and he must reconsider why it happened. This demands maturity from the manager. But a manager is evaluated on the basis of his subordinates performance. Subordinates' zeal is a manager's merit.

Responsibility and authority are intertwined. They must be in approximate balance. Power without responsibility leads to tyranny. "Power tends to corrupt and absolute power corrupts absolutely" (Lord Acton, *Letter to Bishop Mandell Creighton*). Responsibility without power is strangling. A responsible person should be endowed with adequate resources including the information needed to carry out the responsibility. The resources are, however, always limited. The communication cannot be complete either. Power and authority are seldom in a perfect balance. Management is an imperfect art, and it has a great deal of tolerance of ambiguity in it. Managers can acquire authority and power instead of asking for it. It is performance that counts. If someone has exceeded his authority and performs excellently, no trouble will ensue. Poor performance is not acceptable, even if it would be defended by limited authority.

Delegating is very much an individual skill. Some are better at delegating than others, but everyone can learn to delegate. On the other hand, it is also an organizational phenomenon. Middle managers have little room to delegate if the top management does not delegate anything to them. Individual delegating needs a decentralized organization. Profit centers have been organized for many reasons, but one of them is the ease of delegation to them.

Delegating has prominent advantages. Through delegating, decisions are sent to the organization level where the decisions are carried out. People carry out their own decisions better, easier, and more efficiently than decisions of superiors in the organization. Delegation allows people to plan the ways by which the decisions are best accomplished. They know best how to overcome the practical obstacles on the way. Decentralization diminishes the number of organizational layers. Neither jobs nor people are needed whose only function is to control without a value-added of their own.

When delegating operations, a manager can concentrate on her managerial work. Whenever a manager is doing what her subordinate can do, she is neglecting her own job. By way of delegating, a manager can release herself from dealing with what is urgent to what is important.

Delegating is a way of showing trust in subordinates. Most people are worthy of trust. People who are not should be confronted rather than let pass unnoticed. Delegating is a means of encouraging and inspiring people to grow and develop in their job. A developing person is a great joy and merit for his manager. Indeed, this kind of a developing person is no longer a "sub"ordinate, but a responsible job incumbent, who enjoys growing and developing in his job, and he even radiates this feeling around him. Delegating is, for a manager and his subordinate, a process of growing together, in which both parties learn and enlarge the field of their shared experiences.

Delegating has its difficulties, even when sincerely attempted. Obstacles to delegating exist in managers, in subordinates, and in organizations. If one recognizes them, they can be overcome.

There are companies with a tightly centralized management style. The undivisibility of responsibility is sometimes misunderstood to mean that it cannot be shared at all. This may derive from the history of the company. Managers who founded the company from nothing and who went through painstaking phases to get it established may have had to concentrate power at some time in the history of the company to get it established. This habit may be hard to give up when a new phase and the size of the company requires decentralization and delegating. In some organizations, the culture is patriarchal, controlling, or mistrusting. Bureaucratic regulations are a hindrance to delegation. Ambiguous organization structure and job design that are not built on responsibility create confusion in delegating. These organizational hindrances can be overcome by means of organization development. Neglected training and incompetence of personnel jeopardize delegating. Finally, too slim an organization, even though it has many obvious benefits to it, may prevent delegating: there is simply no one to whom to delegate. In this case, automation has given us machines that can do the routine jobs. Can automating jobs to machines be included in delegating? Do we give power and authority to them in this process? Are they going to "manage" people who created them?

Delegating asks maturity, trust, communication skills, willingness to share, leadership skills, even assertiveness when needed. What if the subordinates perform better than the manager thought and even better than the manager himself could have performed? Managers with poor self-esteem may find this positive outcome difficult to accept. No one is perfect. Delegating is risky. A first-timer may do it all wrong, and then it is the manager who has to take charge of the consequences. (Beware, however, those who make no mistakes at all. They are likely to do nothing new at all. It is quite as bad, though, if the same mistakes are made over and over again; it is a symptom that mistakes have not been dealt with properly. One should learn to make new mistakes and more interesting ones all the time!)

By delegating, a manager eases his own workload by giving some of it to others, which helps him to focus on important things. Nonetheless, it is one more paradox of delegating that in beginning to delegate, the delegating itself takes more of a manager's time than his doing the job himself. Namely, he must communicate and guide the delegatee, discuss the objectives and expectations, explain the difficulties that are likely to be met, even exercise control, and perhaps observe in the end that it all went quite differently from, or worse than, what he expected. All this is, however, a learning exercise that saves time later. If a manager is too busy to find time to delegate, he is caught in such a vicious circle that he can cut it only by—delegating.

There are people who as subordinates are unwilling to accept a larger responsibility, but prefer to do only what they are asked to do. They may be very good in operative jobs. But many of them can grow if they are trained to accept authority and responsibility. They may have been spoiled by their former managers and organizations. Having gotten over these earlier fears and experiences, an enormous amount of energy and radiance can be released from them. They feel born again because they are trusted, and they are willing to show that they are worth it. Competence may be an obstacle to delegating, but it can be corrected through training and education.

Personal crises may be a temporary or a long-time disturbance that diminishes the possibilities to carry out job responsibilities.

This asks tact, even flexibility. The possibilities are not limitless, however. Sometimes in personal crises, a manager may be the main or even sole tie of the person to other people. It is, however, of no use that the manager takes the role of an amateur psychiatrist. When a manager sees that this kind of a situation turns from bad to worse, the best service he can do to the person is to advise him to seek professional help.

Delegating is not a collection of tricks and techniques; rather, it involves growing together, sharing together, and learning together. Yet, writing about it is not possible without simplifications. Bearing this in mind, the delegating process can be divided into three over-lapping phases. The first is the assigning of authority and responsi-bility; the second is follow-up on the delegating, and the third is the review afterward.

In the assignment phase, the authority, information, and resources are given to the responsible person. Objectives, expectations, limita-tions, and deadlines are discussed in this phase. The manager's vision and view of the organization and its future helps the delegatee to see his responsibility in a wider context. It is good for the manager to say that he is not interested in how the job is done, but this remains up to the person in charge to decide. The managers can express further that he is willing to discuss any matters that arise, but he expects from the person in charge more suggestions than problems. The manager is willing to share what he knows, but he is not deciding on the delega-tee's behalf. The manager can encourage and stir up the initiative of his responsible person, providing a challenge and a chance to excel. All this is what the manager had better communicate upon delegating—it will also tie him to act accordingly.

The follow-up of delegation is a delicate phase. The manager is still responsible for what he delegated. He is sharing the responsi-bility instead of dividing it away or giving it up; thus, it cannot be indifferent to him how things progress. Yet, it is easy and also dangerous to fall into the trap that despite assigning the authority, the manager begins to watch over the shoulder of the delegatee or to spy on how he performs. The manager should not get mixed with nor correct details as long as all progresses in the right direction. It is wise for him to maintain a distance from the delegated job and its performance so that he remains able to see the delegated job from a wider organizational perspective. The manager is supposed to encourage, support, and help, but he should definitely not decide on behalf of the person who has been made responsible for the job. It is a good practice to agree that the person in charge reports deviations, but this is not likely to be sufficient communication. Unofficial communication is, of course, needed as well. The option always remains that the manager has to withdraw what he delegated in case of an unforeseeable failure. If this is frequent, then the manager had better put his delegating skills under scrutiny.

The review afterward is, unfortunately, often forgotten, even though it is, at best, a most powerful pedagogical experience for both involved parties. It can be done by asking questions such as the following: Was the end-result what was expected? If it was, is it time to tell it to the person in charge and to thank him? If the end result did not meet the expectations, why was it so? What could the manager have done better? Where did the two parties fail to communicate? What kind of misunderstandings occurred? Did someone fail to perform in the expected way? Why did this happen? What can be done to remedy this in the future? Did unforeseen problems appear? Would it be possible to prepare for them better in the future? What was learned from this in all?

Managers often feel so busy that all they can do is tackle projects and problems as they occur, with little time to develop the organization. This is a vicious circle that most probably ends up in individual burn-out and organizational collapse. In the long run, managers are expected to make the organization tick without them.* As true as this is from the point of view of organizational performance, the power plays of organization frequently point to the opposite. In times of an economic depression, managers may become especially defensive to protect their present position, even if this goes against organizational development. Organizational development, nevertheless, presumes delegation and sharing of responsibility widely throughout the organization. This releases management from controlling details to the more vital managerial tasks.

---

*John Maynard Keynes is quoted for saying that in the long run, we are all dead. True as this is, organizations have a life of their own and it may be much longer than that of individuals and at least longer than the individual's stay with the company.

Delegating is a very central managerial skill. Two managerial styles can be discerned on the basis of delegating skills. One is called the piston model of delegating; the other is the pit model.

Managerial layers or vertically adjacent responsibilities can be described by a piston model. The responsibilities are illustrated by a cylinder and a piston that moves up and down in the cylinder. The piston can be in the extreme position of Figure 5.16 only when the lower responsibility is occupied by a person who has taken all of the responsibility—the delegation has in this case been complete.

Whenever a manager has a new subordinate, he must take more detailed charge and guidance of the newcomer's job; indeed, he must do the job with him as this is often the best way to guide (Figure 5.17). Then the manager fills his and his subordinate's responsibility—the cylinder in the model keeps shuttling up and down the piston. As the newcomer learns his responsibility, the

FIGURE 5.16. The Responsibilities Illustrated as a Piston Model

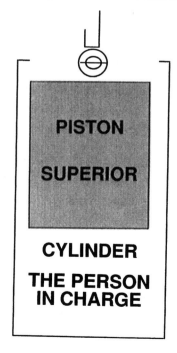

manager delegates to him more and more responsibility—the piston moves up little by little and stays there (Figure 5.18). A mature person even pushes his manager upward. One day the situation in Figure 5.16 has been reached, and the responsibilities have been grown apart. Even then, whenever needed, the piston can descend down, but if this happens frequently, the delegating has failed.

The other way of introducing a newcomer is to leave him alone, let him find out the way to learn his responsibility, and test whether he learns his job. The superior stays in the extreme position in Figure 5.16 without sharing responsibility, without orienting and guiding the newcomer. The newcomer finds himself in a pit (Figure 5.19), from which he has to get out as best he can. The result is

FIGURE 5.17. A New Subordinate

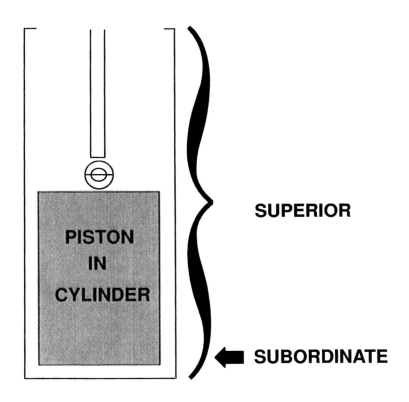

FIGURE 5.18. The Subordinate Begins to Take Charge

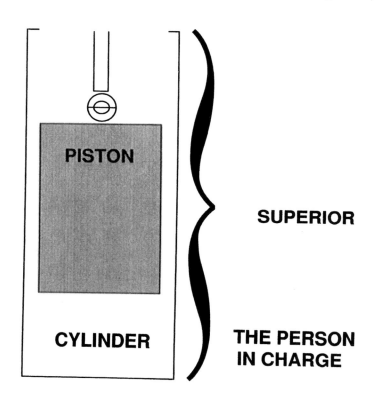

seldom optimal. Some manage; many do not. If there is a job or jobs in a company where nobody succeeds, there is a reason to believe that the job is a pit by its design or by its management.

How to Manage Your Superior

Management literature and management education discuss the superior-subordinate relationship almost from only the superior's perspective. Management is seen as managing subordinates. Delegation occurs from top to bottom in the organization. But managers have their managers as well. The relationship with higher-ups in the organization is frequently felt to be at least as difficult and decidedly

FIGURE 5.19. A Newcomer in a Beginner's Pit

129

more delicate than relationships with subordinates. The first relationships with a superior is to many young people a momentous, sometimes love-hate experience. It may be the beginning of a lifelong relationship to a career mentor—or even a godparent—or it may be a long-remembered disappointment.

In the beginning, a new superior-subordinate relationship is necessarily one-sided. Even though the newcomer has knowledge and professional skill, her knowledge of the organization is negligible, and because of this, she needs her superior's time, support, and guidance.

But in due course, the subordinate is expected to take charge so that she can take possession of her job without asking much advice and authority from her superior. She learns to sell her ideas to her superior, and even to manage him; in other words, she is allowed and expected to influence her superior on the basis of her own job and all the know-how it provides her with. She has to be different from her superior and more competent in her own job; if the two are similar, one of them is not needed. Every job, in order to have its raison d'etre, must have its own value-added instead of being only an echo of what others are adding. A job needs to be more than a faucet that lets things go through as they come without adding any flavor. Being a subordinate does not mean being subservient.

A manager can expect independence, assertiveness, even loyal stubbornness from the ones who report to him. It is not only that subordinates are dependent on their superior, but superiors are dependent on their subordinates, too. The loss of a competent and responsible person causes quite an amount of trouble. This kind of a person is not easy to replace, and it means a potential loss of sales income, clients, or even products. It is perplexing to report about the loss to one's own manager and clients. Power is not a one-way street from top to bottom; it flows from bottom to top, too. It is possible for anyone to influence his manager. Your manager is manageable (Darling and Taylor, 1986).

Not that it is always easy. The manager may not be caught easily. Managers spend much of their time in liaison inside and outside the company; therefore, they may not be available when you need them. Nonetheless, the subordinate has the right to have some of his superior's time. It is better to disturb your superior on an important issue than, say, let him hear your troubles from someone else. It is worthwhile occasionally to reserve time for a more thorough discussion. Performance reviews serve that purpose well.

It is better to have a fair and open discussion than to build a false image that everything goes better than it does. Your superior may be in a better position to sort out some of the problems, and it is, under any circumstances, better for him to know about them than encounter them unprepared. A subordinate's trouble spots are trouble spots for his superior, too. In addition, he has some trouble spots of his own. You had better serve him with your views and suggestions instead of presenting problems only.

Superiors, even the most excellent of managers, are human, and that means they have human flaws. They are as pleased being appreciated and thanked for good performance as anyone else is. On the other hand, flattering, servility, and falseness in general do not take you far, even if such actions would seem beneficial for the time being; in the long run this creates a false relationship that does not help when tough problems are confronted. Clever tricks, cunning and disregarding your superior on matters that are his responsibility have the same effect: it may be possible to manage an issue or two in this manner, but it does not help to create a good relationship. A fair and open relationship works best in the long run for both parties, for the work to be done, and for the whole organization.

What if you just cannot manage with your boss after having done your very best? If the relationship is at stake, so are you and your job. One possibility is that your superior represents the organizational culture, which he has as little power to change as you have. It is possible, too, that he has more experience and a wider vision than you have even if his possibilities, willingness, or skills in communicating it are not good enough to share with you. No one is perfect. You are not expected to love your boss—only to work with him. You might also consider that your superior has a say about your promotion, but alas, it would be sickening to work for a lousy manager for this reason only.

If none of these reasons are accurate, the possibility remains that you have got a lousy boss, e.g., one who is afraid of your competence and considers you a competitor rather than a responsible person willing to take charge. Unfortunately, this kind of manager exists (see Bassman and London, 1993). Possibly, the two of you are just incompatible personalities, whose personal chemistry produces more heat than enlightenment.

If the relationship does not work, and you, other people, and the job suffer from the circumstance, you had better start looking for a new job. There are counselors in the personnel departments in some companies to whom you can talk about your wish to be transferred within the same company. A temporary project may provide an opportunity to show your capabilities. Naturally, the option always remains to find a new job in another company.

REVIEW QUESTIONS

1. Discuss the management activity of organizing.

2. What is meant by a one-man show?

3. Discuss the core ideas of management by objectives.

4. What is the relationship between delegating and responsibility?

5. Discuss typical problems in superior-subordinate relationships and how to overcome them?

LEARNING EXERCISES

Analyze your own job.

1. Which three roles are the most important in your job?

2. Describe your job using the form in Figure 5.14. Use a separate sheet for the purpose.

3. Think particularly about the key result areas of your job. Use Figure 5.11 as a trigger. List three important key result areas below.

4. Discuss the outcome of the preceding exercises with your superior. What did you learn from the discussion? Did it cause some changes in your views?

Chapter 6

Leadership

The high destiny of the individual is to serve rather than to rule.

—Albert Einstein

WHAT IS LEADERSHIP?

A manager can be appointed. Leadership must be earned, even after appointment to a managerial position. Leadership is not a position in an organization, but an active, influencing force. Leadership is not based on a position or status, but on authority and prestige. Leadership may come from personal enthusiasm, personal authority, credibility, knowledge, skill, or charisma; in short, it is derived from the influence that the leader has on his followers (Darling, 1992).

Leadership, then, is a many-sided thing, and it does not render itself into a short, precise, and concise definition. In this chapter, first an account on the nature of leadership is attempted. Then its role in motivating, teamwork, and in conflicts and disturbances is discussed.

Customary definitions of leadership include the following points: setting of values and objectives and leading people with them; having the ability to acquire and organize resources; giving feedback; giving support and trust by delegating; having the determination to reach objectives in spite of momentary adversities; taking responsibility for difficult and critical decisions; standing up for others; being able to resolve conflicts; being a father (or mother) figure; and being able to buffer blows and disappointments (Bennis and Nanus, 1985; Kotter, 1988; Yukl, 1989; DePree, 1987; Javidan, 1991; Sooklal, 1991). There are many dimensions and types of leadership, and leadership varies along with the interaction of the leader, the manager, and the organization (Ropo, 1989).

The previous list of leadership qualities cannot be conclusive. As it stands, it is a very demanding list, but even a satisfactory performance as a leader requires the ability to discern the essential from the less essential. Then, the leader is able to discern the critical situations that call for strong personal leadership. Without this discernment, management is fussing and bouncing around, and the trifle becomes a matter of prestige, while the critical is not decided on due to a shortage of courage.

Here is one more way to try to catch the many facets of leadership. Leadership stands above what is present and, hence, is able to discern what is crucial in the future. This vision becomes a resource in organizational learning to produce human and social capital. This vision is born, changes, shapes itself, and is reborn in the process of organizational learning. Leadership directs this learning process. In this kind of a process, leadership does not define the objectives as clearly as in the case of executive management. The outcomes of the process are as ambiguous as the future itself. However, leadership increases the maturity of the organization to cope with the future—whatever it will be. A leader needs much more tolerance of ambiguity than "pure" management. Leadership is straining and exhausting; it asks for tenacity and the ability to absorb shocks, more so than management, which is protected by position. Leaders go through career and personal crises. Lähteenmäki (1993) shows that companies are poorly prepared to handle crises.

In conclusion, there are managerial positions and managerial work conducted in the positions, while leadership is not tied with a position, but it is a behavioral phenomenon that makes people and organizations function better. Without the latter, a waste and even a blockade of human resources in organizations take place. These resources are not released by way of statements or manifestos only. Leadership involves assertiveness that does not necessarily benefit the leader, but takes personal risks, commitment, and responsibility for difficult situations amidst conflicts, risks, and ambiguities. Even a steel fist may exist in the silk glove of leadership. If it is needed frequently, however, power has replaced leadership.

Leadership may be for better or for worse. Conger and Kanungo (1988) write about the often-forgotten darker side of leadership as well. In literature the positive consequences are well elaborated, but for example, Hitler fulfils many characteristics of leadership. Without leadership, morally valuable reforms cannot be achieved either. This is why leadership is closely connected with ethics. Treatises on business ethics have become abundant in recent years (e.g., Pastin, 1986; Cadbury, 1987), but still, leadership ethics have remained a widely neglected area of study. The media have been more active in publishing flaws in leaders' ethics.

This kind of leadership approaches the type of strategy discussed at the end of Chapter 3, which emphasizes strategic learning of the whole organization. Especially at times of great transitions, the two become close to each other. Leadership was treated in early leadership literature (e.g., Katz, Maccoby, and Morse, 1950) mainly as a subject for the middle management and supervisory levels. Now, however the concept of strategic leadership (e.g., Schendel, 1989) has highlighted how close strategic and leadership issues are at times of great changes. This is also one piece of evidence to show that categories such as strategic management, managerial work, and leadership are more or less arbitrary, though needed for expository purposes.

MOTIVATING

Engineers define the performance of a machine as the product of its capacity and energy. Human performance can be defined respectively (Figure 6.1, cf. Vroom, 1964 and Porter and Lawler, 1968). The human capacity is related to knowledge, skill, know-how, i.e., cognitive factors of behavior. The human energy is reflected in

FIGURE 6.1. Motivation and Performance

$$\text{PERFORMANCE} = \text{CAPACITY} \times \text{ENERGY or ABILITY} \times \text{MOTIVATION}$$

$$\text{MOTIVATION} = \frac{\text{PERFORMANCE}}{\text{ABILITY}}$$

motivation, the will to do, i.e., the dynamic factors of behavior. In other words, motivation is the energy component of behavior.

Motivation and capacity are not additive in the formula. Instead they are multiplicative. This relation implies that if one factor of the product is zero, the performance is zero. Without motivation, even a high capacity amounts to zero. The formula is, admittedly, misleading so far that, in fact, the combination of a high motivation and little capacity leads to mischievous consequences (the busybody syndrome).

Yet, the utilization of human capital in organizations is restricted rather by motivational concerns than by shortage of capacity. It is not often that people get exhausted because the work it too demanding for their competence. Much more often, people get fed up in their work due to frustrations, i.e., due to the feeling that the work is not meaningful and does not match with what they could do. Interpersonal and organizational frustrations block much energy. Motivational constraints are caused by multiple reasons, and they are rooted deep down, on the one hand, in the organization, its management, and culture, and on the other hand, in the individual personality and consequently, in where the two meet. Troublemakers are seldom incapable people. They are often capable people who feel they are restricted to use their capacity properly and constructively. They may even work as channels of pollution of the whole organization and its nauseating atmosphere.

People are by their very nature energetic. In that sense, motivating is not needed—it is there already. Motivation is a culture-bound phenomenon. Western people, in particular, find it inconvenient to stay lazy for long—though the massive unemployment in many European countries in the 1990s certainly influenced motivation and morale. People who are considered lazy in their work can be tremendously active in their hobbies. Motivation, or the level of arousal in physiological terms, varies between people. Each individual has his own optimal level that he tries to maintain. Exceeding this level is stressful, and normally a person tries to reduce it back to his optimal level of arousal. A too low level of arousal is boring, and a person will find something to do to raise his level of arousal. The form of the function between the level of arousal and performance is seen in Figure 6.2. The level of arousal improves the performance but only up to a point. After this point, the perfor-

FIGURE 6.2. Arousal and Performance

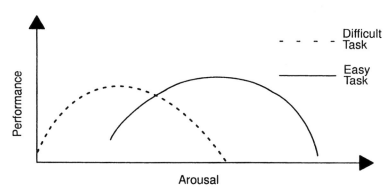

mance is steadily impaired. The level of difficulty of the perfor-mance affects the level of the culmination point. Cognitively com-plex jobs are performed better at a lower arousal level than routine jobs. As the level of arousal increases, people move by a physiolog-ical necessity to a more routinelike behavior. From this follows a managerial predicament: busy and stressed managers find it diffi-cult to concentrate on cognitively complex issues, not because of their incapacity, but because it is difficult for them to reduce their level of arousal to a level optimal for the purpose.

People need not be motivated—they have motivation by their very nature. People direct this motivation, or level of arousal physiologi-cally speaking, toward the kinds of objectives they find preferable. These *motives* or directions where the arousal is aimed at are either inherited or learned, and they make people aspire to their objectives in socially regulated ways. The question that confronts managers is, how to get the arousal and motives of people directed in a productive way for the organization. There is no simple answer to the question, as anyone who has worked as a superior or a subordinate knows. It is not possible to motivate or manipulate anyone at another person's will. Arousal and motivation can be developed or suffocated by means of management. They exist in every human being without pressure from superiors. There is no way or trick to give motivation to a person from the outside if it does not meet the intrinsic motivation of a person.

Theories of motivation abound, and they belong to the most quoted material of textbooks, e.g., Timm, Peterson and Stevens (1990). Maslow (1954) and Herzberg, Mausner, and Snyderman (1959) are among the most popular ones. The former describes needs as a hierarchy of physiological, security, social, prestige, and self-sufficiency needs from the lowest to the highest needs. Herzberg dichtomizes the needs into extrinsic needs (hygiene factors) and intrinsic needs (motivators). The former refer to the working conditions outside the job and the latter to the work itself. It is the basic assertion of Herzberg that hygiene factors may be a reason for dissatisfaction, but even when they are as good as they can be, they only minimize dissatisfaction, but do not give rise to a positive motivation to work. Only the motivators, i.e., an interesting and challenging job, are conducive to a real work motivation.

Figure 6.3 illustrates the point of Herzberg's two-factor theory as a result of a survey that was conducted in an in-house course for managers. The participants were asked—as in the original study by Herzberg—to mention their most positive and most negative experience at work. The distribution of the answers in the figure shows that the majority of positive experiences were associated with the motivators (the upper part of the list), whereas dissatisfaction was associated with the hygiene factors (lower part of the list). It is the work itself that produces or fails to produce motivation. The extrinsic, administrative factors increase or decrease dissatisfaction. Motivation and dissatisfaction, accordingly, are not ends of the same dimension. They are caused by different factors; they are two different dimensions, and they are influenced by different means.

Criticisms have been leveled against the Herzberg theory on the grounds that it may apply to intellectual work only and that it is the product of its methodology to ask for critical incidents rather than a genuine distribution of factors that influence motivation (e.g., Schneider and Locke, 1971). It is true, too, that in some respects, the two-factor theory may be more modern than at the time of its inception nearly half a century ago as a consequence of structural changes in the economy and the nature of work. There has been a great wave of automation in industry, in retail trade, and even in many parts of administration, and we have not seen all of it yet. A new wave is going on along with developments in information technology. As a result, many jobs that require manual, mental, or social skills have been replaced by a fewer number of jobs with more monotonous work. It is difficult to see how these jobs could

FIGURE 6.3. The Distribution of Satisfaction and Dissatisfaction in a Finnish Company Classified According to Herzberg's Factors

		Satisfaction (+)	Dissatisfaction (−)
Intrinsic factors or motivators	Achievements	31	7
	Recognition	25	3
	Interesting job, increased responsibility	5	
	Advancement, professional development		2
	Σ	61	12
Extrinsic or hygienic factors	Company policy and administration		32
	Supervision		8
	Working conditions		3
	Salary	2	
	Status		
	Relationships with subordinates	4	4
	Relationships with colleagues	3	
	Relationships with superiors		17
	Safety		
	Σ	9	64

be intrinsically interesting and challenging. A manager who tries to persuade the worker to believe so comes to be considered a manipulator rather than a motivator.

There are some possibilities to increase the variety in these kinds of jobs. Work rotation is one often-used means, and it is useful, because it increases flexibility of the organization and replaceability of people. However, its possibilities remain limited. Basically, people do dull work for their living, and they do not imagine then that they can realize their potential in the work. Even the fear of losing one's job is an incitement to work harder. It may sound somber that there are jobs where, and people to whom, survival and other extrinsic factors are the only reasons to work. But there have always been these kinds of jobs, and the ongoing automation is producing more of them. People's interest in these jobs is first and foremost in the salary that the company pays for their living (see Lähteenmäki and Paalumäki, 1993). Their motivation is instrumental: the work and the pay for them is an instrument for the quality of life outside work. In terms of Herzberg, it is the hygiene factors that count in these jobs and for these people.

At the same time, there are jobs that are impossible to be automated. In service industries and in the knowledge-intensive sector in particular, new ones arise. People in these jobs value the professional ethic oftentimes more than the organizational culture, and they perform best when driven by their intrinsic motivation to do a good job. These people cannot be managed and motivated by hygiene factors; they work for intrinsic motivators.

These kinds of jobs and people are found in traditional industries, too. The service sector abounds with them despite the automation and bureaucracy contradicting motivation. Maintenance work is difficult to automate, and there are lots of new possibilities for skillful, craft-based, and professional people in fields such as housing and industrial maintenance at a time when real estate is aging. Many companies have outsourced their maintenance services, which has created new entrepreneurship opportunities in the business. In personal selling and in consulting services, a person who is well versed in his product, service, and clients cannot be replaced by a machine. An enterprising and capable person develops in these jobs the competitive edge of the business. If she is not satisfied with the company, it is not too difficult for her to find a job in another firm or even to found a company of her own. In this situation, the intrinsic motivation is the key.

Motivation cannot be donated nor transferred to another person. Nonetheless, there are organizational means to influence it. It is well-known that a great amount of personnel turnover and absenteeism are symptoms of organizational diseases that diminish motivation to work for the organization. Personnel turnover and absenteeism result in more costs than most companies realize. Other symptoms of poor motivation are more difficult to measure, but they can be noticed by anyone who walks around organizations with open eyes and ears. In the following, a few means to influence motivation are discussed.

The challenge of and interest in a job can be increased by way of job design. When a person can plan his own work, get feedback of how he is doing compared with his plan, and, in this way, is in control of his own work, he finds it more meaningful. Figure 6.4 presents a checklist that provides ideas to design and enrich jobs into meaningful entities based on the trinity of planning, operating, and control. Objectives work as challenges. They help a person to see his progress, so he need not rely on the feedback he may or may not receive from others. Too modest objectives, as well as ones that are believed to be unrealistically high, motivate little. The possibility to plan one's own work usually diminishes the dissatisfaction that is caused by poor organizing.

Of course, compensation affects satisfaction, as does the basis for and system of compensation. The use of incentives has become widespread, and the experience gained is mostly positive and on many occasions very positive. Incentives are not easy to apply in all jobs, and

FIGURE 6.4. A Checklist for Analyzing Meaningful Work

Plan	Do	Control
Can the individual or group –have customers and delivery dates for services –set goals and standards for the job in the frame of company policy	Does the job –require human talents or attention –consist of making a comprehensive product, semi-product, or part of a product	Can the individual or group –get feedback of how well they are doing –know quantity, quality, and cost requirements
–state the product quality and quantity requirements	–enable seeing the relationship of the job	–influence quantity, quality, or cost factors
–have possibilities to state resource requirements	to other operations and to the context of the whole company	–identify and correct conditions that affect quantity, quality, cost, and safety
–know cost and feasibility requirements		–get information by their own records or from elsewhere to evaluate performance

if they are arbitrary and they are not based on performance, the arrangement often raises more problems than it solves. Compensation has instrumental value outside the work. It is also used and felt as a grading device of the importance of jobs (see Delacroix and Saudagaran, 1991). Compensation is considered a measure of success in work, but there are cultural differences in the value attached to it.

Compensation is not, however, the one and only factor in satisfaction, motivation, and performance that it is sometimes thought to be. It is just easier to complain about compensation in public than about some other more delicate factors. In fact, some people have changed from a managerial position to jobs that are lower paid merely because they wanted a less stressing job.

Poor equipment and working space make people angry and even mad, yet they can also become status symbols. They are typical extrinsic factors that may produce dissatisfaction, but even at their best, they produce little motivation, unless the job itself is rewarding.

People desire to be appreciated. People who perform well are worthy of being appreciated. Cultures differ in the ease of giving thanks for good performance. Yet, everyone likes to be thanked for a job well done. The western parts of the West are much better at it than the eastern parts. Americans are sometimes considered overwhelmingly sweet and informal in Eastern Europe, while Eastern Europeans may be considered blunt and blatant by Americans due to a different communication pattern. In international business, differences in communication pattern have already caused more than considerable misunderstanding.

Possibilities to progress in one's work and career are certainly challenging. Competition evokes conflicts and impedes cooperation, too. Competition is part and parcel of a market economy, and it is prevalent inside companies as well. Yet, the cooperation, communication, and interaction within a team are major competitive advantages. The proper mix of competition and cooperation is another delicate task for managers to create and maintain. Many present-day organizations are much too big for individuals to identify with; therefore, an identity with one of its parts, units, or departments could give a sense of belonging to a group. This identity with the group could give a sense of cooperation within the group and a sense of competition with other groups in the same corporation. Team bonuses as a means of compensation support this sense of togetherness. This sense of belonging to a group makes it easier for an individual to see his contribution first to the group and through this to the corporation, to society, and to the common good of humankind at large.

TEAMWORK AND TEAM LEADERSHIP

Teamwork as a Form of Cooperation

Teamwork may have two kinds of objectives: coordination and innovation. They may, at first sight, appear to be incongruent, but in fact, they can be combined at the same time. Researchers of creative work have concluded that creativity is, to a great extent, an ability to combine opposite things and processes (see Ford and Harris, 1992). Both divergent and convergent thinking are needed in creativity.

Much too often the rigidity and formality of the line organization, its power, and reporting relationships accentuate the vertical interaction in the organization at the cost of the horizontal communication. Teamwork is one measure to open horizontal communication and to add to the elasticity of the entire organization. In a functional organization, the functions are interdependent, and they need continuous coordination. Objectives and performance reviews give a basis for coordination. When this has been done, teamwork may be most helpful to make the objectives shared.

Trainers in creativity have found teamwork to be a splendid instrument of innovative thinking. Innovation can be exercised in all teamwork. The presence of a team increases the level of interest and prompts new ways of thinking. Novel ideas are oftentimes strange combinations of two or more old ones. Also, different persons with different backgrounds can help create something new, something that is more than one person could have created before the teamwork. This is synergy or the "1+1=3" effect.

Teamwork is not the panacea for cooperation problems. Poor application of teamwork corrodes individual responsibility and decision responsibilities. It is possible to waste time and get on people's nerves by teamwork that leads to nothing. Teamwork has been used for the purpose of burying things instead of getting them decided. Teamwork has been used as a camouflage of autocratic management. Hidden agendas in the meetings may make it impossible for the team to reach conclusions. Teamwork can slow down decision making if decisions are not allowed to be taken by individuals or if people do not have the courage to make them without the express acceptance of a formal team meeting. Nonetheless, teamwork can also be utilized as a superb instrument for innovation and coordination. It can also be said that teamwork can be applied properly or improperly. Teamwork does not prevent managers or organizations from failing. In order to add some value, teamwork has to be managed properly; it needs to be built on a responsibility-based organization, simple rules of conduct, and skill in teamwork (Darling and Taylor, 1989).

The first social psychological laboratory experiments late in the nineteenth century dealt with the effectiveness of teamwork. The question then was, Which is more effective, a group or an individual? The results were and continue to be contradictory. On some occasions, the group improves; on others, it impairs individual performance. There is no law of nature to determine the effectiveness of teamwork. It is up to team leadership to make the team perform by getting the resources of the team out in the open, building them up for a synergistic outcome, and even reinforcing the team resources by way of team learning.

In present-day companies and in modern management, teamwork is a necessity. A functional organization requires teamwork for the coordination of departments, as none of them alone can be responsible for the performance of the whole unit. Teamwork facilitates management and leadership, and properly conducted, improves communication and saves time for all concerned, as many issues can be dealt with while everyone concerned participates in the meeting. Teamwork has motivational meaning as well. In organizational development and in in-house training, teamwork has established itself as a major educational resource.

Teamwork in companies is often structured. The teams have a leader and roles, objectives, accountability, schedules, deadlines, and other characteristics of task forces. Teams are organized as management teams, functional teams, project teams, committees, quality teams, production teams, etc. There is no point in asking whether teamwork is productive or not. It has come to stay. The point is how to lead it in a productive way. This is the subject of the following.

Team Leadership Styles

For the purpose of illustration, let us assume that a team has a problem to solve, and the team consists of three members: person A who has control of 50 percent of the resources (expertise) needed to solve the problem, person B who has 30 percent control and person C who has 20 percent control respectively (Figure 6.5). Let us assume further that the resources of the members are not overlapping and that they are additive. Then the team as a whole has 100 percent of the resources needed for the solution of its problem. In this instance, all individual solutions remain inferior to the solution in which the group manages to combine its resources. The case is ideal for teamwork, but it requires team leadership skill to get the members' resources out in the open and to get them combined in a joint solution. The task is simple in mathematical terms. Anyone familiar with teamwork knows that it is not as simple as that in organizational terms.

FIGURE 6.5. A Fictional Team

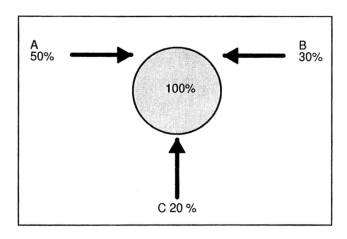

The example is a simplified one, but it is by no means alien to everyday teamwork. For instance, in budgeting, the expertise of marketing on demand, production on resources and capacity, and finance on cost and feasibility considerations need to be combined. These three duties belong to different persons in the organization. They are complementary, though, and admittedly they are usually somewhat overlapping and not as simply additive as in the fictional example. There may be social, managerial, organizational, and political factors in play that do not appear in the example, which is reduced to the basics. The reduction, however, illustrates the essence of teamwork and serves the present purpose. The example is used to illustrate the difference between four team leadership styles. The styles are dictation, compromise, integrative, and synergistic teamwork.

Dictation Teamwork

In this team leadership style, one person dictates the outcome of the team, and the rest have no contribution to it whatsoever. This could also be called autocratic leadership style. The outcome in the fictional example is 50 percent at best when A is the dictator. At worst, the outcome is 20 percent when C is the dictator. In this leadership style, the team can undermine the outcome from what it would have been, if the best or even the second best individual solution had been accepted.

In fact, no teamwork has taken place. One person has just echoed his views in the group, or his team leadership skills have not sufficed to bring the others' resources out in the open. Unfortunately, this kind of a situation is not a product of imagination only. Of course, it can be an efficient way of informing, in case no contribution from the team is expected.

Compromise Teamwork

In a compromise, a dispute is arbitrated; an "average" solution is sought for in a solution that approaches the middle of the team members' views. In the example, the average is about 33 percent. Again, it undermines the best individual solution. By way of bargaining, the second best choice has been reached.

Compromises are fairly common, even though the outcome remains below the best possible. Sometimes the resources, expertise, or convictions are either additive nor measurable, or they are different in quality or built on values about which no objective, "right," optimal, or maximal solution exists. Compromising may also be attempted when a consensus, arbitration, or holding of the group together is more important than its performance. This kind of an occasion occurs especially in political and value-related disputes.

Integrative Teamwork

In this kind of team leadership, the resources of the team are gathered together into an integrated outcome of the team. It sounds so very basic and simple. In fact, it is not simple at all—it requires active leadership, active listening, acceptance of different views, ability to present one's view and to change it on the basis of communication with others, ability to objectify issues irrespective of who holds them, dilution of status and prestige, and time and patience to get all the resources into the open and integrated into a fair outcome. The list is not conclusive, but it suffices to show the difficulties encountered in integrative teamwork.

As difficult as this style is, it has much more potential than dictation and compromise can ever have. It is a learning exercise for the team members: the resources of the team members are now greater than without and before the teamwork as they have all gained in learning from each other. Integrative teamwork makes the 100 percent solution possible. The team has added value. In this style, the different views do not divide people; rather they pose a problem that the team members share. Integrating is time consuming, but the time spent in it has a better return than in dictating and compromising. It is possible to learn integrative teamwork. This learning diminishes time needed for the integrative outcome.

Integration is not, however, always only positive in its consequences. There is evidence showing that in well-integrated teams, the members may share not only their resources, but even their blind spots. Janis (1972) coined the concept "groupthink" to point out the inability of a cohesive group to see and accept critical and optional views. Groupthink has been shown to be a factor in major catastrophes and fiascoes, e.g., the disastrous failure of the space shuttle Challenger, when it exploded soon after it was launched (Moorhead, Ference, and Neck, 1991).

Synergistic Teamwork

In synergistic teamwork, the team creates something new and more than the addition of the individual resources would be. The outcome is something that no team member possessed before and without the teamwork. This was developed in the process of teamwork, when the combination of the members' resources exceeded the input. In creative work, views are combined in a unique way, and this is precisely what synergistic teamwork is about. It could be called innovative teamwork as well.

In synergistic teamwork, the outcome exceeds the 100 percent of the input to the teamwork. This is the most productive style. At the same time, it is the most rewarding to the team members. Synergistic teamwork is of paramount importance in knowledge-intensive organizations, but it is not an easy style to apply. Sweeney and Allen (1984) studied teams of excellent performance. They observed that these kinds of teams did not come into existence as a result of intentional management, but they seemed to grow spontaneously from a fertile breeding ground. The breeding ground can be developed by management, but apart from that, management has little to say in igniting the process nor getting it to sparkle once it has been started. These innovative, synergistic groups were characterized by a high level of enthusiasm, motivation, commitment, experimenting, an inside jargon that the outsiders found difficult to understand, the fusion of work and leisure, pride in the team, and indifference to rules. It also appeared that these kinds of groups did not maintain their level of energy for long, but in due course, they tended to dissolve as spontaneously as they appeared.

Relatively stable high-performing teams have been observed in artistic team performance. Murnighan and Conlon (1991) concluded that successful string quartets have learned to live among conflicts and paradoxes and even to absorb them as a part of their artistic performance. See Figure 6.6 for a summary of team leadership styles.

FIGURE 6.6. Summary of Team Leadership Styles

The style of teamwork	Result
Dictation	20 to 50 percent
Compromise	33.3 percent
Integrative	100 percent
Synergy	> 100 percent

Uses of Teamwork

Management Teams

Management teams (Figure 6.7) represent an application of Likert's (1961) team management concept. Management teams are used widely in management practice. They are built on the organization and its reporting relationships. They consist of a manager and those who report to him. A manager belongs to two teams: the one he leads and the one that is led by his own manager. Managers are linking pins between the two teams and the respective layers of the organization.

Figure 6.8 exhibits rules of a company executive team. The company has respective rules for functional management teams and for supervisory teams. The rules leave ample room for interpretation and are adapted liberally.

Functional Teams

Functional teams are useful in organizations with interdependent functions. This kind of a team is a very flexible channel for direct communication and interaction and prevents communication running only to or via the first common superior. So, the research and development function needs to share what happens in the market, what manufacturing can produce, and perhaps even what can be

FIGURE 6.7. A Network of Management Teams

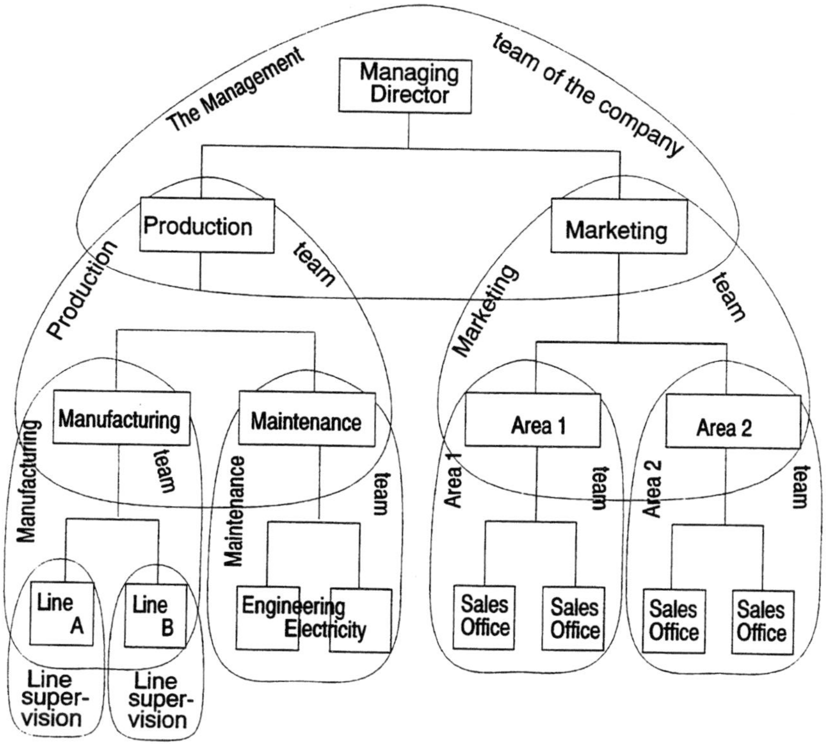

FIGURE 6.8. A Specimen of the Rules for an Executive Team

FICTION LTD.
THE RULES OF THE EXECUTIVE TEAM

1. General

The executive team ascertains that:
- plans and decisions are discussed and thought over from many angles;
- production and marketing are coordinated and serve the objectives of the company;
- the communication is efficient and flowing in all directions.

2. The Members

The executive team consists of the Managing Director (the Chairman), the Director of Production, and the Director of Marketing. The meeting is recorded in minutes, which consist of the decisions, persons in charge of their implementation, and the deadlines of their implementation.

3. Working Procedure

The executive team is not a drafting or planning committee. Things are accepted on the agenda only when they are ready to be decided upon. Even if the issue is not ready to be decided, it is delegated to the person in charge of its implementation.

The members of the executive team can delegate the implementation of the decision of the team to members who do not belong to their executive team. Even then, its member is in charge of his job as authorized in his job description. The executive team integrates responsibilities, but it does not reduce individual accountability.

The executive team meets once a month unless otherwise agreed.

In addition, it may gather together for longer meetings to address specific issues.

---

financed. A product and development team serves this purpose very well (Figures 6.9 and 6.10). A logistics team is another case in point, as logistics is entwined with other functions (Figure 6.11).

Project Team

Project teams are set up for steering project organization. Projects come and go whenever the need arises. Projects are disposable orga-

FIGURE 6.9. An Example of a Product Development Team

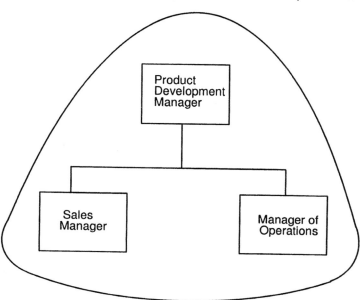

nizations; they are set up for a specific task with specific objectives, and they are dissolved when they have completed their task. Being temporary, they ventilate and go beyond established structures and, all in all, add to the flexibility of the whole organization. The project team meets to evaluate the progress of the project against its objectives and to steer and program into its next phases. Many committees, temporary teams, commissions, and the like could be steered as project teams, but their work is seldom programmed as carefully as in ongoing projects.

Production Teams

Production teams are a means to organize the operative work. They belong to the formal organization and, in a way, are the special cases of management teams, in which the trinity of planning, operating, and control have been reduced to the operative level. In clerical work, this kind of an organization is used as well. Production teams are sometimes called semi-independent, autonomous, or self-managed teams; these terms emphasize that the teams control themselves within the framework of objectives (see Kulisch and Banner, 1993). Production

FIGURE 6.10. An Example of a Product Development Team

THE RULES OF PRODUCT DEVELOPMENT TEAM

1. General
   The Manager of Product Development is in charge of product development. He works all over the organization collecting ideas and finding out where and how they can be implemented. The work is discussed in the project-development team, which supports the Product Development Manager in order to coordinate product development with the objectives of the company.

2. Tasks of the Team

   - to discuss ideas and determine the ones for further development;
   - to discuss research proposals and research results and recommend further research or decisions to begin manufacturing for the executive team;
   - to make proposals to develop product-development function;
   - to support the Manager of Product Development.

3. The Members
   The Manager of Product Development (the Chairman), Sales Manager, and the Manager of Operations.

4. Meetings
   Meetings once a month upon the request of the Manager of Product Development.

---

teams are related to job enlargement and job enrichment: when a job that includes the planning-operating-controlling sequence is too large for one person to manage, a team responsible for it is set up. The representatives of teams may gather at determined times to discuss and make suggestions for improvement (see example reported by May and Flannery, 1995). The quality teams or quality circles have been applied mostly and best by the Japanese, though they, in fact, imported the idea from the United States, where it was promoted more widely than before the Japanese initiated their practice (Deming, 1986). The introduction of production teams tends to create a greater transformation that requires changes in the physical site, production technology, and—not least—in the minds of people.

FIGURE 6.11. A Logistics Team

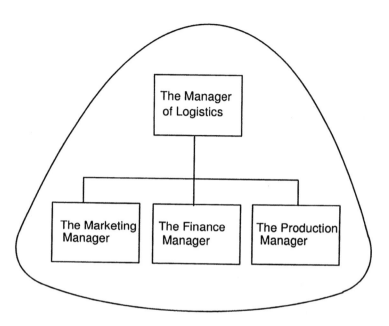

Innovation Teams

Innovation teams are used for the express purpose of creating new ideas and innovations. Creativity is an aspect of all teamwork; nonetheless, specific teams for this purpose are sometimes needed. Special techniques for innovation and creativity include brainstorming and collective thinking.

Training Teams

Training teams have become popular in all training and education. Teams can determine solutions to prescribed, structured problems. They can, likewise, exercise teamwork, interpersonal or leadership skills, or other social skills by means of process learning.

CONFLICT MANAGEMENT

Conflicts and Troubles Are a Part of Management and Leadership

The anecdote has it that a King educated his Crown Prince with the following words of wisdom. Remember, my son, life is not dancing on the roses only—it is also pomp and circumstance. This does not apply to managerial work.

Managerial work is not dancing on the roses either. It is among other things managing conflicts, disturbances, troubles, and unpleasant, discomforting, and repulsive issues. A manager is expected to take care of what others are not able to do, and the above list notes one category of them. A manager is not expected to delegate the awkward issues and leave to herself the easier ones. A manager is expected to focus on what is important, not on what is nice and easy to do.

A manager's job is to ask, even demand, performance from herself and from others. She must stress economy and economizing—and it is not always a pleasant job. She must see to, speak for, and guard the advantage of her organization, which is apt to lead to conflicts of interest with people that she has nothing against in person. It is far from pleasant to reject ideas, even excellent ones, that are not in line with the demands and possibilities of the company at that time. Criticisms against the organization are disclosed to the manager, even if it may be painful to hear and to act upon—but, notwithstanding, necessary and useful to do. Discovering faults in others and reproving them pleases few, but it is not entirely unavoidable. Admonitions may be necessary. Dismissing people is among the most onerous of all managerial duties, especially in cases in which the people have done good work and may have nothing to do with the reasons for their being dismissed.

Controlling and inspecting are necessary parts of managerial work that many managers do not like. It is not possible for a manager to withdraw himself to major issues only; he must, by necessity, spend a considerable part of his time in dull routines. The work requires indifference to personal relations in cases in which subordinates and clients rightly expect the same rules to apply for all. You can make friends in business, but you cannot make business of friends. The role in work may be in conflict with other roles (Darling and Cornesky, 1987).

It may be best to manage a conflict as quickly as possible. Terminating individuals is painful, but it may cure. You had better not worry what has to be done although, admittedly, this is easier to say than to follow. However, there are also conflicts of which time will take care of, and it is better not to rush to solve every minor problem. Organizations are never perfect; they do not sound like symphony orchestras but rather like jazz bands with improvising soloists and pitch distortions.

There are a few commandments on how to give criticism:

- Criticize the point, not the person.
- Do not criticize a person, particularly a subordinate, in the presence of other people.
- Be specific.
- Present a criticism soon after the fact.
- Discuss the consequences of the fault and what can be done to avoid the fault in the future. Then forget the whole thing, and do not mention it again.

Classes of Conflicts

Conflicts do not burst out by mere chance or by the ill will of people. They are caused by incompatible interests or by incompatible views of the parties involved. On this basis of the two classes of causes, a dichotomy of conflicts can be presented. The first class consists of irreconcilable interests, or cases in which the conflict is about dividing a benefit. The second class consists of contrary views, or cases in which the interests of the parties do not clash, but the ways of seeing it are too different for mutual understanding.

In practice, the two classes are not that distinct, but they may go together. So, there may exist a wide discrepancy of views about the means to gain benefits for the organization, but, once this problem is solved, a conflict of interests about how the benefit is distributed may follow. Nonetheless, the two classes are different enough to be treated distinctly for expositional purpose.

Conflict of Interests

In a conflict of interests, one party can gain only at the cost of another. The sum of the gains and losses of the parties is zero. A zero-sum game is a classic model of conflicts of interest. The conflict is rooted in the structure of the situation, and it is not possible for the parties to eliminate the cause of the conflict. Most central debates of theories of society and schools of social perspectives concern this kind of chronic conflict. There are two main ways to handle an irreconcilable conflict. One is to try to extinguish it; the other is to regulate it. Karl Marx had much to say about extinguishing, and the regulation theory has been promoted by Dahrendorf (1959), in particular.

There are many ways to try to extinguish a conflict. Denial, undermining its significance, and persuasive communication may all be used as a means to prevent the conflict from coming into the open (Sitkin and Bies, 1993). Force and violence are more extreme means. They do not work forever when the conflict is structural and its reasons keep on generating disagreement. It is possible to cover and defuse the conflict for some time, but a conflict of interests tends to smoulder, aggravate, and finally emerge again to the surprise of all who thought it was already extinguished. Extinguished structural conflicts of interest are the best fuel for underground revolutionaries and terrorists.

Regulation is the other way to handle conflicts of interest. The regulation cannot eliminate the causes of the conflict either. Instead, the regulation attempts to influence its manifestations and to build an arena where the conflict can be discussed openly. The regulation presumes, according to Dahrendorf, three conditions: (1) acknowledgment of the conflict by both parties, (2) organization of the parties, and (3) agreement on rules about how do deal with the conflict.

The debate on conflicts of interest has been most intense on the macrolevel of society. However, they exist within organizations as well. An organization is an open system, and in its exchange with its environment, it receives its share of social conflicts. Yet, there are also conflicts of interest inherent in the organization itself. Investment decisions, compensation, and promotion of people are example issues in which conflicts of interest exist.

Conflict of Views

Nonetheless, many conflicts that we meet in organizations are not reducible to conflicts of interest. Misunderstanding, opinionated views, communication distortion, and many other muddles in the daily toil produce cross winds and conflicts. These kinds of conflicts of views are created inside the organization and its administration. Poor communication and information breed misunderstanding, especially in that rumors fill in what is not known. Ventilation of views prevents seeds of conflicts from increasing.

Conflicts of views can be eliminated by confronting them. The confrontation means that the conflict is faced and dealt with out in the open by all parties concerned. In a confrontation, the causes of the conflict are openly addressed. Then, the parties can discuss how to approach the matter and eventually attack the causes of the conflict. By confronting and eliminating the causes of the conflict, the conflict itself can be eliminated. This is the only way to eliminate a conflict.

In a way, the confrontation of a conflict is reduced to problem solving. By discussing the causes, the conflict is thoroughly examined; tenable reasoning is accepted; untenable reasoning is rejected, and entirely new angles to the conflict are learned. The solution is the integration of the conflicting views into a new organizational innovation. This process of conflict resolution coincides with integrative teamwork and the creativity in it. A confrontation is not only a way of troubleshooting but, in the end, a rewarding process that aids the performance of the organization. It is not an easy process to go through, however, and often a third party can be very helpful in conducting it.

Conflict resolution is not a matter of learning to use tricks, quick fixes, or panaceas. It may not necessarily work as an isolated project that focuses on the manifestation of trouble only. It is oftentimes a starter to a comprehensive organizational development process.

The types of conflicts and their resolution attempts can be illustrated in a classification model (Figure 6.12). Extinguishing conflicts of interests and views tends to reinforce negative consequences of the conflicts. The causes of conflict generate pressure (Figure 6.13) that bursts out one way or another, even if the regulation or confrontation

FIGURE 6.12. A Classification of Conflicts

Type of conflict

		Conflict of interests	Conflict of views
Mode of treatment	Suppression	Aggravation	Demoralization
	Admission	Regulation	Confrontation and resolution

FIGURE 6.13. The Pressure Model of Conflicts

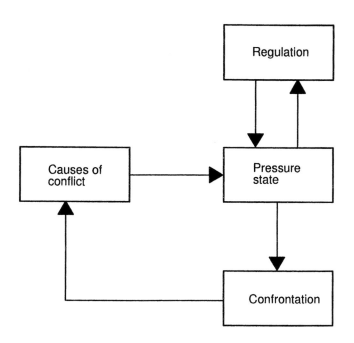

have been blocked. The regulation levels off the pressure so that it is manifested in peaceful forms. Confrontation can eliminate the causes that generate the conflict and, by so doing, reduce the pressure or eliminate all of it. This latter option, though an optimal one, is not easy to attain.

Conflict Resolution

Conflicts are unavoidable. We must tolerate, survive, and live with conflicts. Conflicts are not only a disturbance, but they may also be an impetus for individuals and organizations to grow. Quinn and Cameron (1988) stress that paradoxes and transformations go hand in hand; participation, innovativeness, and propensity to change correlate with conflicts (Figure 6.14). Conflicts arouse participation, and participation brings forth conflicting views. Conflicts, when properly treated, are innovative and increase the propensity to change, but there is no reason to paint a pretty, romantic picture of conflicts. They may be accompanied by individual tragedies and organizational fiascoes. Conflicts are avoidable, and it depends on conflict resolution whether their net outcome is positive or negative (Darling and Cornesky, 1987; Jehn, 1995).

Unanimous nonconflict dominance in an organization can be effective, at least in the short run. It goes straight and fast like a train crushing small obstacles on its way. But too homogenous an organization is unable to turn quickly. A group of people that has stayed unanimously stable for long is not prepared for abrupt changes; it is in the groupthink trap, which is short of alternatives and self-criticism. Organizational conflicts and paradoxes, even their dysfunctional elements, are imports from conflicts and paradoxes in the

FIGURE 6.14. Some Contingencies of Conflicts

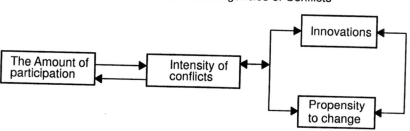

environment (see Smith and Gemmil, 1991). One day some of them take over in the environment and resonate inside the organization if they have been allowed to exist there. In our era of abrupt and unpredictable change, an order without conflicting elements is not viable. Experimenting with wild ideas and even a fair amount of chaos shake established routines, increase the will to change, and prepare the organization for transitions.

To remain viable and transforming, organizations need a proper amount of tension. For example, the varying time spans of functions create tensions. Research and development aim at excellence in the future, whereas manufacturing needs to get its product delivered before a particular deadline. Marketing needs to look at the markets of the future while salespeople need to make money today. There are built-in conflicts in a functional organization. It is good to confront them at times not only to let pressure be released, but to seize the opportunity for organizational development. Confrontation meeting (Figure 6.15) is an excellent instrument for the purpose.

The confrontation meeting of Figure 6.15 was conducted in a middle-sized engineering company. In its first phase, the department teams got together to discuss and jot down what they expected from the other departments. Their list in Figure 6.16 is not an uncommon one in a functional organization. After this meeting, the department teams were told that other departments had produced corresponding lists about them, and the teams now had to discuss and write down what they thought these expectations to be of themselves. In the third

FIGURE 6.15. The Agenda of a Confrontation Meeting

1. What do we expect from others in groups?

2. What do the others expect from us in groups?

3. Sharing the two points above together.

4. What can we do to facilitate the cooperation in groups?

5. Sharing the former point together.

6. How do we proceed?

FIGURE 6.16. Departmental Tensions in an Engineering Company

Assessor \ The object of assessment	Administration	Product Development	Production	Marketing
Administration		Insufficient coordination of research Isolation Product ideas are not treated in a systematic manner Obstinate standardization Poor product management	Poor quality control Primitive purchasing Inadequate delegation Undeveloped storage bookkeeping Training is not planned	Inadequate planning Poor budgeting knowledge Inability to delegate Fickle sales policy Agreements are not kept
Product Development	Insufficient information Ambiguity of organization Inadequate product cost accounting Poor organization of catering Clocking-in procedure		Unwillingness to make prototypes Inadequate resource information Poor quality Resistance to develop manufacturing methods Purchasing lives from hand to mouth	Careless in technical matters Poor information from clients to product development Ignorance of the sales policy Poor expertise in products Needless rush
Production	Poor information Inadequate personnel policy Consider themselves superior Intangled files Withholding cost data	Isolation Rigidity Fuzzy responsibility Dependence on one man Are adamant not to change anything in their drawings		Poor expertise in products Interfering purchasing Idiotic rushing Selling products that cannot be made Incomprehensive instructions in special deliveries
Marketing	Delaying delivery Poor pressing of claims Poor information Poor statistics Slow internal mail	Make product changes that do not suit the clients Do not listen to marketing when designing new constructions Secrecy about designs No information about new products Old-type registration	Slowness Deadlines are not met Constant dissatisfaction of special products Undeveloped work planning Poor quality control	

phase, the teams met together to share the lists. In the fourth phase, the department teams, each on their own, discussed and wrote down what they could do to make the interaction go more smoothly for the joint performance. Finally, the teams met together to discuss and decide upon the latter suggestions. The meeting resulted in a better understanding by all the participants and also suggestions for new organizational arrangements that were introduced later.

Vertical confrontation meetings deal with the relationships between managers and those who report to them. In all, by means of this kind of horizontal and vertical confrontation meetings, clogs and plugs in organizational structure can be opened for better performance of the whole organization.

REVIEW QUESTIONS

1. What is leadership? How is it different from management?

2. Discuss the relationship between motivation and performance.

3. What is synergy in teamwork? Discuss.

4. Discuss the functions of a management team.

5. What are confrontation meetings? How can they be a positive influence in leadership?

LEARNING EXERCISES

1. Answer the following.

   • Describe incidents in your work when you felt particularly satisfied.
   • Describe incidents in your work when you felt particularly dissatisfied.

2. Classify your preceding answers into the classes noted in Figure 6.3.

3. Do your answers fit with Hertzberg's two-factor theory? Compare your answers with those of others.

4. Make up a team of about five persons. Work out a suggestion about how the performance of teamwork and the motivation of the team members can be improved. The suggestion must be completed in half an hour.

5. Next, assess your teamwork by going through the following questions.

The Goal

- Did you state the goal explicitly?
- Did you remember the goal while discussing?
- Did you revise the goal during the discussion?

The Program and the Timing

- Did you program your meeting beforehand?
- Did you revise the program during the session?
- Did you keep to the program?
- What caused the deviation?
- What did you learn for the next session?

The Leader

- Did you have a leader?
- Should the team have had a leader?
- Did the leader direct the discussion?
- Was the leader too dominant?
- Did the leader facilitate the interaction?
- Did the leader shut others' mouths?
- When and where did the leader inhibit the interaction?
- When and where should the leader have been more active?
- What did you learn for the next teamwork?

The Interaction

- Did the interaction flow evenly and comprehensively?

- Were there some people who dominated the interaction?
- Did cliques appear?
- Did you keep to the agenda? If not, did it matter? In what way?
- Was the interaction open and sincere?
- Were conflicts brought into the open?
- How were the conflicts dealt with?
- Did you pay attention to conflicts?
- Did you listen to conflicting views?
- Did you decide by the majority?
- Did you vote?
- Did you compromise?
- Did you avoid conflicts?
- What did you learn from the next teamwork?

How Would You Characterize Your Teamwork?

- Dictative
- Compromising
- Integrative
- Synergistic

Chapter 7

Management of Change

When one has come to terms with himself, he finds less to fear or dislike in others.

—Author Unknown

TRANSFORMATION LEADERSHIP

This book began with a vision of Moses. Now we will soon enter the third millennium A.D. There is, clearly, something everlasting in management and something contingent to the times. Change is neverending. What is changing all the time are the means to make the organization keep beat with the tune of times.

Each era tends to see itself as more unique and dramatic than it is, when viewed from the distance of time. Having said that, it is very obvious that companies are going to encounter in the foreseeable future continuous discontinuities. Instead of changes, we had better speak of transformations—instead of a continuous change, companies need to change from one form to another.

Well, this has happened, and this is happening all the time. Companies have moved from one business to another; the ownership arrangements have reshaped entire industries, and fusions have merged companies into others. In cost-saving operations and organizational shuffles and reshuffles, downsizing of companies has taken place. Companies have been transformed or have suddenly even ceased to exist.

Nevertheless, we may have seen just a prelude thus far. Competition is only beginning to be global. European integration, whatever its future form and details will be, affects its members and outsiders alike. The Japanese industries have competed successfully with the Americans in the latter's strongest areas, including the automobile and electronics industries—and they are very strong within Europe now. But do not think that Americans have been beaten. All this means an increasing need for strategic management to see the role of the company amid the changes, intensified managerial work to get it all done, and leadership to make the transformation happen. The competitiveness of products, prices, quality, and design are not enough. What is needed is competitive management. It is only now that international management leadership is becoming the competitive advantage.

This book has described this kind of competitive management or transformation leadership from the following different angles:

- strategic management that helps an organization learn to create a future outlook that endures and changes by reacting to and creating transformations
- managerial work that is responsible in carrying out this outlook today
- leadership that brings the outlook alive in people and in what they do

The three perspectives meet in strategic leadership (Figure 7.1) that helps people do the right things and, by so doing, makes people live and review their outlook for the future in their daily work.

Does this sound difficult? It is difficult. But it is the future toward which management and leadership must develop, at times succeeding, at times failing, but still maintaining its course and direction. This kind of management becomes a competitive advantage of a company.

How can companies develop management toward this direction? There are two interdependent dimensions of this: individual managers and the organization above, under, and around them. This is the issue to be addressed in the remainder of this book. The first question is, What managerial skills need to be developed? Second the special individual factors in internationalization are considered. And, third, developing and transforming the whole organization are discussed.

FIGURE 7.1. Approaches to Management

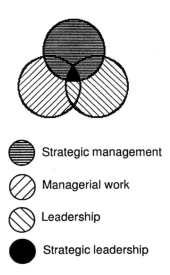

Strategic management

Managerial work

Leadership

Strategic leadership

DEVELOPING MANAGERIAL WORK

What is a good manager like? This is the question of questions. So many management books and courses raise this question, yet no universally accepted answer is available. Kurt Lewin's field theory from the 1930s suggests that all behavior is the function of the person and his environment. This notion has captured the debate on managerial effectives. Sometimes personality factors, sometimes environmental (situational) factors have been emphasized.

A whole host of empirical studies have evolved to determine personality traits that correlate with management and leadership skills (see Ghiselli, 1971, for a pertinent example, and House and Baetz, 1979, for a review). From the 1960s on, situational factors were given more weight. More recently, both are credited, and the interaction and the interrelationship of the two have been considered decisive. A manager has a margin of environmental and situational constraints and possibilities within which her personality can operate (Schreyögg, 1980).

The best-known theories that gave prominence to personal qualities of managers are trait theories. Biographies and autobiographies of managers promote the "Great Man" theory, implying that the leaders they describe have had some inherent great qualities (e.g., Iacocca's 1984 autobiography, and Sherman's 1989 account of Jack Welch). Leadership-style theories, which were extremely popular in the 1960s and 1970s, consider style a more or less individual behavior that could be developed by means of training. In spite of a huge amount of research, the results have not shown what personal traits differentiate effective managers from the less effective ones (House and Baetz, 1979). The effectiveness of leadership styles is considered contingent on situational factors (Reddin, 1970), and a flexible style proves more effective than any dominant style.

As there did not seem to be a stable correlation between the traits of managers and their effectiveness, researchers turned to situational factors for an explanation. The most extreme position was suggested by the group of researchers and consultants in the Strategic Planning Institute (Schoeffler, 1980). They concluded from a vast data base that the profitability of a strategic business unit is almost exclusively dictated by markets, irrespective of the management of the unit. The 1980s and 1990s have proved this view wrong. Within one and the same industry under the influence of the same market forces, there were and are great company-specific and management-specific differences (cf. Thomas, 1988). This holds true despite the fact that until now there have been industries in which management as a competitive advantage has not been tested. When the competition grows more intense and global, the role of management must grow from what it had been.

It is time to return to the equation of Lewin and give the person and the situation their fair roles. The situation certainly influences and sets a margin for what a manager can do. In different situations, different kinds of management are needed. For example, during a boom, management can be assertive, growth oriented, even aggressive, while during a depression a more defensive, cautious, cost-conscious style is a must. Situations select managers—and they test them as well. But the fit between an organization and its environmental situation is facilitated or inhibited by a flesh-and-blood manager. Then, the questions follow. What kinds of qualities does a manager need to be able to help her organization adapt to the environment, but also to influence the environment in a way that is favorable to her organization? What is required from a person to work as an effective and transactional agent between the organization and its environment?

The international competitive environment is going through a great and unpredictable transformation. Internationalization brings new dimensions of change. In this transformation, a manager can change his personality, but only within limits. Then, the ability of a manager to make a fit between his organization and its environment is a stable quality in managerial performance in the continuous, discontinuous transformation. The following catalog of the qualities of this kind of a transformational manager is based on interviews with managers (Nurmi, 1987).

Possess a Strong Personality

Even though the personalities of high-performing managers are most variable, they all share a strong personality by which they have the impact they exercise on their organization and its environment. It gives the manager the credibility in the process of bringing the organization and its environment together.

Get Along with Other People

A manager must get along with other people. This includes delegating, communicating, and motivating. This is not only, nor even basically, a matter of techniques, skills, traits, styles, or other special characteristics. It is more basically a matter of being a mature adult; this includes acceptance of others, communication without biases, and an active aspiration toward confidence, honesty, and high ethical values. Credibility, consistency, predictability, and openness in communication can be listed under this heading as well. This all sounds like more than one person can ever reach; the point, though, is that a manager is expected to strive for this end.

Discern Essential from Less Essential

A manager must be able to discern what is essential from the less essential. He needs to see through what is the core and soul of the organization and find the policy line to be followed. It is from this that visions and strategies grow. This has been called "helicoptering": a manager must ascend to see the whole picture, but he must also be able to pick the place and time to descend quickly to a detail that needs to be addressed.

Make Decisions

A manager must make decisions, quickly if needed, under difficult, ambiguous, and risky conditions. In addition, she is expected to stand by her decisions and be an example for others in following them. Decisions are the results of managerial work, and managers stand or fall with them. One major incorrect decision can overthrow a manager; indeed, it can be fatal to the whole organization. Examples are not so rare. An inability to make decisions, however, is among the greatest faults of a manager. Risk is a concomitant of all decisions among the uncertainties of the world that we live in, but it is no excuse for deferring decisions whose time has come.

Possess Drive

A manager needs drive; she has to be hungry for results and push her organization forward. It is not sufficient for a manager to perform well for the time being; she needs to make her organization perform better in the times to come. In that sense, every manager is an entrepreneur.

Possess Integrity

These points enumerated thus far reflect a pattern instead of traits taken one at a time. A person with this kind of maturity, drive, and perspective gets along with others, has the integrity to discern the essential from the hustle and bustle of the day, and can carry out what has been decided. Integrity is more important than the addition or combination of individual traits as such.

How can one develop toward becoming this kind of a manager? Management is so difficult that no one can be perfect at it. In the following, suggestions for management development are presented.

The list cannot be complete or universal; it is meant as a trigger for a self-analysis.

Orient Yourself and Your Organization to the Future

The challenges of the future give meaning to you and your people's work. Beware not to get stuck in predicaments of today of which time will take care.

Do the Important Before the Urgent

Admittedly, this is not easy advice to follow. Nonetheless, being too busy in the routines of the day may prevent you from seeing and setting priorities. Being busy all the time and doing what comes to the surface next leaves little time to think of priorities. Without priorities, you keep yourself busy in doing whatever arises. This is a vicious circle. It can be cut only by setting priorities and sticking to them. It is more important to do the right things than to do something right.

Communicate, Communicate, and Communicate

A manager receives much information that others in the organization do not get. Communication may not be simple, particularly when the information is not documented, but is a part of the managerial experience and contacts. Even then, it is communication that adds to the possibilities of more shared communication. This requires redundant communication and tolerance of misunderstanding all the same. In international business, learning to communicate cross-culturally is a particular challenge.

Delegate

As a manager has always more work than time and other personal resources to do it, he has to divide his work and share his responsibility with others. Jobs cannot be divided haphazardly. A most important resource for performing a job is information. In poorly divided jobs, people are required to spend time asking for information or not performing well because of a shortage of information moreso than if the job had not been divided at all.

Use Other People

It is not possible for any manager to master everything. It is good to learn to work with people who can consult and advise in the area of their expertise. In big companies, such people exist in staff positions. Another possibility is to use outside resources (lawyers, consultants, trainers, colleagues, friends, etc). Just talking with an outsider may be helpful.

Realize Your Own Influence

Managers have more influence of an indirect nature than they often realize. What a manager says and does may be considered to have more meaning than intended. It has a symbolic value attached to the managerial position, and it influences the priorities and time management of others. A joke, a careless remark, or a thought presented in passing may have effects that the manager never realizes.

Learn from Obligations

A manager has many duties and obligations. She can make this necessity a virtue and learn from her obligations. They provide an opportunity to create contacts and learn from them by giving and taking.

Accept That You Cannot Be Perfect

Managers have too much work to be able to reach perfection in all of it. Therefore, many issues must be managed as routine or even superficially. This leaves time to get versed in what is really important. In order to be able to do this, you must have your priorities properly determined.

Find Time to Develop Yourself

Even though, and particularly when, the problems of the day are pressing, managers must find time to look after their own professional and personal development. It is everyone's right and duty to do so. Do not expect other people or your organization to suggest it, but take the initiative in your own hands. If you do not, you are, in fact, running fast into the obsolescence trap. Managerial and leadership skills and the special techniques required to be a good manager must be brushed up now and then. Inherent in this point is refreshing yourself as a person—body and spirit.

SPECIAL REQUIREMENTS
OF INTERNATIONAL MANAGEMENT

All of the previous suggestions for management development are important in international managerial jobs as well. In addition, cross-cultural skills are needed. There are considerations that relate to a geographical area, the job, and other specifications. In the following, some rather general considerations are examined. Their emphasis varies considerably in different cases. The following catalog is based on the authors' experience and Heller (1980), Mendenhall and Oddou (1986), Phatak (1989), Zeira and Banai (1985), Tung (1982, 1987), and Ronen (1986, pp. 529–535).

Experience

The old recruitment rule of thumb says that nothing predicts future performance better than past performance. There is some basis to this rule in international recruitment as well. There is, also, a chronic shortage of people who have extensive experience in international management. Recruitment, then, is often based on past experience in the recruit's native country only. After all, even experienced people have had to start without experience. However, a long but narrow and one-sided experience may be even a hindrance to learn new ways of thinking and acting that are needed in a radically different environment.

International experience, even living abroad for a period, is educating and widens one's views. Even a substantial international experience is no replacement for professional experience and industrial experience. Managerial experience, work experience, interpersonal experience, organizational experience, and experience in life at large are facilitators in the active adaptation in a new environment on one's first international job. Even then, surprises will follow.

Education

Education of one kind or another is often seen as a requirement for an international assignment. Recruiters certainly pay attention to it. The degree gives credibility in addition to the knowledge and skills one may have gained through experience. A degree is also a test passed by the person showing that he has determination to learn. For young people with limited experience, the degree may be the only proof of their capabilities that they can show in a recruitment interview. It is common that a foreigner is recruited because the host country is short of people with professional education. In an international assignment, there are so many new things to be learned that little time is left to learn the profession if one has not previously learned the profession. The subject of the education is specific to a job, but the point remains that a good education helps one acquire an international job while aiding job performance.

Language and Communication Skills

English is considered the lingua franca of business. This is an oversimplification. It is possible to buy anything in almost any language, but in selling and marketing, the one who knows the client's language has an advantage. The knowledge of Spanish, French, German, Chinese, and Japanese is a great asset in doing business, particularly in countries where these languages are spoken as native tongues. Even if you know a little of the language of a country where you are doing business, your attempts at using the native tongue are appreciated, and this will help you to acquire contacts.

The different communication patterns, verbal and nonverbal, in different cultures are not easy to discern; therefore, they produce considerable confusion at times. Americans are usually very free and easy in meeting persons for the first time, while the French and the Germans, in particular, expect a more formal introductory meeting. In English, thinking aloud is common, while in the Finnish language, what is said is meant to be more solid and factual, almost a promise; no wonder, the English may consider Finns to be blunt, whereas the Finns believe the English to be unreliable. The Japanese find it difficult to say "Oh!" as in their parlance it would be insulting and cause whomever it addressed to lose face. The roundabout expression they would use instead, "It is an interesting idea," sounds almost like "Yes" to a Westerner. It is impossible to avoid a mix-up due to culture-specific communication patterns totally, yet homework pays to sensitize anyone to the most important issues.

Family

Research studies indicate that family reasons top the list of reasons for cutting an international assignment before its completion or before the contract was due (e.g., Tung, 1986, Kauppinen, 1994). Usually this reads that a man has been recruited, but his wife and/or children have found it difficult to settle down in a foreign culture. The role of women varies enormously in different cultures, and particularly women with career aspirations of their own have little chance to live the way they used to in a culture that is very different from their own culture. Leaving friends at home and having few opportunities to find new ones in new surroundings may be hard for the spouse and children in any family.

The duties of a homemaker are likely to be much more demanding abroad than at home. Many things that were easy back at home (such as finding pure water to drink, food without health risks, reliable household employees) may be quite complicated. Homemaker's social duties for the organization may be frequent and on a high level.

For children, living abroad may be a most rewarding experience. It will affect them all their lifetime. They have the chance to learn another language by a natural method without the effort that learning a language later in life always takes. Children are able to accept many things as they are without the conscious adaptation that their parents have to go through. However, an acceptable level of education for children may be difficult in some countries. Health risks and deficient health services for small children also pose a problem in some places.

In all, going abroad is a family matter. The family may support and learn together, but it may also have problems adapting to the great change (see Thornton and Thornton, 1995; Brett and Stroh, 1995). The choice to go abroad is a family choice. Some companies interview the spouses of the candidates and even screen candidates on the basis of their spouse. In other companies and in many countries, the decision is left to the candidate, and the company intruding in family decisions is taboo.

Age

The age of the candidate is a factor in recruiting, but a proper age is a function of many variables. There are reasons to select a young person in some cases; there are also perfectly good reasons to select an older person in some cases.

Younger persons, in general, adapt easier to new conditions of life. Their motivation to learn is typically higher, and it definitely helps them to learn the many things that a new job in a new country presupposes. Language skills and international attitudes are more widely distributed in the younger generations than in the older ones. A company that selects young people for international assignments is also training a cadre of international managers for the future.

Older people supposedly have more experience and maturity. Many families find it easier to go abroad only after the children have left home. There are cultures that stress seniority, and in them, a younger person has difficulty receiving the respect that a senior gets (see Magnusen, 1995). The Japanese appreciate seniority, and for them, the age of a company representative signals status and also the appreciation that the sending company gives to the business relationship. Hence, they may not take a smart, young person in earnest.

Motivation

A high level of motivation is necessary in a foreign job. A person who has been sent against his will or who was drafted to a job abroad may develop the motivation on the spot, but without it, he cannot perform satisfactorily. There are motives to go abroad that predict disappointments and poor performance. Escaping problems at home is one of the worst, and idealistic perspectives about exotic excitement, traveling, and seeing the world, are also poor motives. Working in a managerial job abroad means working hard, and most of it is far from romantic.

The willingness to learn is a very good motivator. This is what international jobs give ample opportunity for—although the learning is not without growing pains. The learning often transfers to whatever one does later in life, especially since everything in the future is going to be more international than today. International managerial jobs usually provide well-compensated salaries and generous allowances. In addition, tax reductions and lower costs of living are in many cases beneficial. This is a legitimate reason for satisfaction, but, as we learned from the treatise on motivation in Chapter 6, a financial reward does not necessarily work as a motivator in the same way an interest in a challenging job does.

Cultural Adaptation

The willingness and ability for cross-cultural empathy are most germane to working abroad (Clarke and Hammer, 1995). Empathy begins with an awareness that values are outcomes of socialization and that the socialization process has fostered different values in different cultures. The way we see the world is not objective, but socially conditioned. This awareness helps us to understand values that are different from our own. Nobody can, nor is asked to, reject his own cultural assumptions, but the acceptance that the others' cultural values are as well-based as one's own facilitates adapting to a different culture.

Flexibility and Resilience

Even the most broad-minded and unprejudiced person is going to confront unexpected surprises when settling down in a new culture. Hence, flexibility and resilience belong in the traveling kits of anyone who has to work internationally. This must not mean giving up the key objectives of the job to be done or the very reason of being sent abroad. In insisting on performance, a manager must be flexible in approaches and the culture-specific ways for objectives to be reached.

Frustration Tolerance

Frustration tolerance is tested when working abroad. Things just do not work out the way they do back home. Working in a country with a less-developed infrastructure is especially trying. And when things go wrong, the best advice is to take it easy; the worst action is to lose your temper and to blame the problem on the locals. This will certainly make things worse.

Delegating

Delegating becomes more difficult in an international setting due to the misunderstandings that so easily occur in cross-cultural communication. Add to this the widely different experiential backgrounds of people who are raised in different cultures, and you have a major example of the delegating dilemma or the imbalance of needed information and what can be communicated. Quite often, a manager mistrusts the skills and competence of a foreigner more than those of a countryman. Nonetheless, delegating is a necessity. In addition to what was discussed in Chapter 5, the law in some countries presumes that certain strategic decisions must be submitted to an indigenous person. Delegating is also a means of training the local people in managerial responsibility and company policy. Besides, the local people know better the markets, habits, culture, recruitment possibilities, and local business environment in general.

Physical Fitness and Health

Physical fitness and health need to be taken care of in international assignments. Climate differences, psychological stress, different food and eating habits, and hygiene conditions may cause bodily symptoms that lengthen adaptation from a few weeks to much longer periods. Also, there may be some minor health problems that cannot be lived with as easily in difficult countries as at home. Vaccinations should be taken care of at home rather than in a country where the health care system is not known or is known to be unreliable. Learning about the local health care is one of the first things that a newcomer must do.

ORGANIZATION DEVELOPMENT

It is obvious that international companies are heading for turbulent times, during which the present business, the present organization, and the present way to manage will have to be changed.* All this implies that successful companies are going to look quite different from what they are now, as the 1990s come to a close. The companies that are not able to go through with this kind of a transformation process will simply lose the edge and give way to the ones that have the necessary ability to transform.

The key concern for this kind of a transformation to be successful is the ability of the organization to learn (see Dodgson, 1993, for a theoretical review). This includes the learning of individuals, but it is a more penetrating organizational process than just individual learning of knowledge and skills (see Slater, 1995). Organizational learning has taken place when the whole company is responsive and resilient to the continuous and discontinuous transformation impulses from the company's environment.

The Dilemma of Transformation Program

The need for organizational learning is beginning to be generally accepted by the managers of progressive companies. Nonetheless, the concept is not an easy one to apply, and there are considerable difficulties in making it happen (see, e.g., Ford and Ford, 1995). This kind of endeavor requires management resources, energy, and time, at the same time as the intensifying competition drains the energy from the management even in the short run. Time is management's most scarce resource, yet no permanent transformation can occur unless management is actively involved. If top management sticks to the problems of the day while the future of the company requires a thorough transformation, and if management also stretchs itself too thin for the future while the battles of today must be won to ensure the company's future, then management remains caught between Scylla and Charybdis. Any transformation

---

*This section is based on the following article: Nurmi, R. (1992). Corporate transformation: A Scandinavian example of a "middle of the road" approach. *Leadership and Organization Development Journal* 13(5): i-v.

program must sail between the Scylla of short timespans and resource involvement and the Charybdis of long timespans and involvement.

There are well-known, well-designed, and ambitious development programs that aim at changing the company by projects that cover the whole of the company. Huse (1989), presents a list of such programs. After the initial enthusiasm, there is a great probability for these kind of programs to die out, simply because the present day problems do not render enough time and other scarce resources for this kind of a program. Another solution for management is to send key individuals for short and superefficient courses to give them the latest knowledge and skills, the fads and fashions of the day. The outcome of this approach seems to be next to nothing as individual learning alone and organizational teaming, even moreso, require a prolonged exposure in order to mature and manifest in organizational behavior.

The program presented here attempts to avoid the Scylla and Charybdis of corporate development by using a middle-of-the-road concept. This is not a compromise, however. The program focuses on the essential cornerstones of corporate transformation, and it does not consume too much time. It is made up of three modules, which extend over a year and are each three days long. These nine days require top management involvement, with the staff working together in analyzing the predicament of today as well as determining the vision on the horizon, and building bridges between the two. The first module adds to leadership skills; the second develops the organization; the third concentrates on strategic management. Individual homework and corporate development occur between the modules. The whole pattern is illustrated in Figure 7.2.

The design intention of the program is (1) to promote learning by doing and reinforcement in classroom sessions; (2) to analyze the predicaments of today, determine the vision of the future, and begin to develop a bridge between the two; and (3) to go through both of these stages to assist the process of corporate transformation.

It is also possible to implement the program in a reverse order. It would be advisable for a company that is heading for a foreseeable business transformation to collect its top management to discuss the strategy first. For the strategic change to be implemented, it must be

FIGURE 7.2. The Corporate Development Program

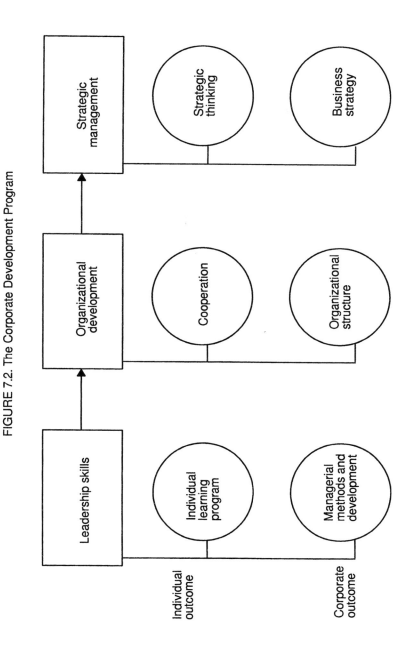

adopted by the organization. For this purpose, the organization development phase is needed. The new organization cries for better management, which can be achieved by developing leadership skills. There are many companies with brilliant strategies on paper, but the implementation of the strategies in practice does not succeed without special interventions in organization and leadership.

The program is based on experiences gained in a fairly large international company that went through a period of long and successful growth. There were some black clouds on the horizon, however, partly due to the management style that was no longer suitable for the size of the company (and indeed the employment of a new chief executive officer) and partly due to the changes within and internationalized competition. Due to these factors, a course in the basics of management was introduced. During and after this course, the need for organizational development arose, and during the organizational development phase, the need to reassess the business strategy and process of its formulation arose. What follows is a general form or a prototype, which will vary in detail depending on the situation of a specific company.

Leadership Skills

The first phase is to develop leadership skills of individual managers (Figure 7.3). It is a thoroughgoing principle of the first module that what is learned can be adopted immediately without organizational or strategic constraints, though at the end of the program, organizational problems are discussed briefly as a preparation for the second module. After the module, the participants are given homework in order to develop their leadership skills. The company's homework is to check its performance and potential reviews with the special emphasis on the communication between managers and their subordinates.

In our case company, the enthusiasm was at its highest after the first module as it opened some vertical communication blocks. After it, a round of superior-subordinate reviews were held and changes in the responsibilities of persons were introduced. This all resulted in a situation in which the whole organization structure was considered obsolete. For the purpose of restructuring, the second module was developed.

FIGURE 7.3. Module 1: Leadership Skills

MODULE 1: LEADERSHIP SKILLS

DAY 1

Morning	Management as a work
Afternoon	Leadership
Evening	Self-management

DAY 2

Morning	Self-awareness
Afternoon	Knowing yourself as a leader
Evening	Delegation skills

DAY 3

Morning	Problem management
Afternoon	How to manage with your boss
Evening	Management of change

Organizational Development

The second module is organizational development (Figure 7.4). This module will vary from company to company even more than the first phase due to the organizational problem spots of different companies. The point is to confront the functional and behavioral problems of the company.

This is a most delicate phase and requires special professional skill from the training facilitators. It is by the same token a most rewarding phase. It releases organizational energy from unnecessary friction to support the mission of the corporate whole. There are blocks and plugs in every organization, and when they are opened, energy flows and creates a new thrust and willingness to work for the company. After the phase, the participants have homework to develop the interpersonal skills, and the company checks its organizational structure.

FIGURE 7.4. Module 2: Organizational Development

MODULE 2: ORGANIZATIONAL DEVELOPMENT

DAY 1

Morning	Job description
Afternoon	Teamwork
Evening	Listening and communication skills

DAY 2

Morning	A diagnosis of the organization
Afternoon	Interdepartment confrontation meetings
Evening	Corporate business unit cooperation and confrontation meetings

DAY 3

Morning	Line and staff cooperation
	Role-play exercises
Afternoon	Organization structure
Evening	Organizational change

In this case company, the second phase led to a major restructuring of the whole organization. The new CEO seized the opportunity to make the organization his own by adding some anarchy in it, by insisting upon individual achievements and disregarding the ways in which they were attained. This created some problems in middle management, and some people were moved horizontally from line to staff positions. These lateral arabesques did not work out well, though. The waves are still rolling.

Strategic Management

The third module, or strategic management, focuses on the business of the corporation (Figure 7.5). Its pedagogical outcome for the participants is the enhancement of their strategic thinking and an increased sensitivity of the corporation as a whole. This, of course, helps the managers discern the essential from the less essential, as well as the contribution of the individual activities to the corporate

FIGURE 7.5. Module 3: Strategic Management

MODULE 3: STRATEGIC MANAGEMENT

DAY 1

Morning	What business are we in?
Afternoon	The cornerstones of success of the company
Evening	The strengths of the company

DAY 2

Morning	Weakness of the company
Afternoon	The mission of the company
Evening	The strategic plan of the company

DAY 3

Morning	Plan for the next year
Afternoon	Change management
Evening	Review of the whole program and what to do in the future

---

mission. During this phase, top managers gain new business ideas and an increased acceptability of change. After the module, the participants have homework on strategic thinking, leaving top management to reflect and reconsider the business and strategy of the company as visualized for the future.

In the case company, the new CEO and his staff enjoyed this phase very much. It provided them with the chance to tell each other what they considered to be key concerns in the business of the company. The earlier strategy had been more on paper than in action, and now the key people shared their business ideas and developed a belief in working in line with it. The implementation—as it seems now—has not taken place quite as well as anticipated because the new business plan was vetoed by the owners of the company on the board. This has hampered the project, but it has not jeopardized its focus. It has also created some trouble for the CEO. As a newcomer, he was in an ideal position to commence the project in an unprejudiced manner. Yet, the owners obviously wanted him to implement it a bit slower. The project is now moving again but at a slower pace than scheduled. On the other hand, the changes in Europe during the past few years have changed the strategic situation of the company considerably; hence, a new assessment is again needed.

REVIEW QUESTIONS

1. What are organizational transformations?

2. Discuss the qualities of good managers.

3. How does one develop as a manager?

4. List at least five requirements that are special for international managers.

5. Discuss the modules of a corporate development program.

LEARNING EXERCISE

Read the following case very carefully. Think about it. What is essential in it? Analyze the state of the company. Put yourself in the role of Dennis Nichols as the newly appointed General Manager. Think what changes are needed. Think how you can accomplish them best. How do you manage this transformation?

Nichols Cattle Feed Company

Michael Nichols 1960–1980

Michael Nichols started a cattle feed business in 1960 by purchasing fodder and forage from farmers in his area; adding protein, minerals, vitamins, and sundry extracts to it; and selling the mixture back as cattle feed to the same farmers. He had a big truck that left his farm loaded with feed and came back loaded with fodder and forage. This was the beginning of Nichols Cattle Feed Company, which during the 20 years of Michael Nichols' reign became a well-known company in its county and a profitable business for its owner.

The company developed a highly positive image in the county due to the good quality of the feed and due to the personal visits that Nichols paid to his customers. Consequently, the volume of the company grew steadily.

In the late 1960s, Nichols recruited two important assistants, Mr. Healy, a young accountant, and Mr. Brown, a technician, for maintaining and repairing of the facilities of Nichols's plant and farmhouse.

During the 1970s, the smooth growth continued, even though Nichols deliberately applied brakes to the growth as he saw that the full utilization of the potential would have increased his own burden, requiring more administrative effort and bringing new financial problems without necessarily adding to the profitability.

In the late 1970s, Nichols employed his elder son, Dennis, as a salesman, then his second son, John, as a purchaser, and finally his daughter, Sheila, as a bookkeeper. The company remained, however, essentially a one-man business in the sense that Michael Nichols made all the business decisions alone and the others remained his assistants.

William Nichols 1980-1988

Michael Nichols died suddenly in 1980. His wife had little to do with the company; Dennis was 20, John was 18, and Sheila was 17. The family asked Michael's brother William, aged 58, to take over for a period to give Dennis some time and experience in the company before he could take over as the manager of the company. William Nichols agreed, though very unwillingly. He was a stationmaster in the Federal Railroad Company from which he was expecting his pension soon, and additionally, he had little knowledge or understanding about the cattle feed business, or any commercial activity for that matter. Realizing that the company would probably be lost to the family without his help, he decided to accept the leadership and resigned his railroad job.

From 1980 on, the market development was very favorable for Nichols Cattle Feed Company. The demand for cattle feed increased. The good image that Michael Nichols had built for the company spread beyond the boundaries of its native county, and new clients emerged without the slightest marketing effort. The volume of the company grew fourfold in the period, and the upper limit was set only by the impossibility of increasing capacity in the present site. Also, profitability grew favorably.

During this period, Mr. Healy turned out to be highly valuable for the company. He did the calculations; he handled the cash flow; he introduced new, simple systems for budgeting and control; he suggested the recruitment of new persons when needed. William Nichols learned to rely on his opinion completely. In 1984, Healy persuaded William to make arrangements for a relatively substantial investment, the building of a new plant for the company.

Also during 1980 to 1984, Mr. Brown became interested in developing new feeders and watering devices for cow- and poultry-barns. They were quite innovative and aroused interest in the local farmers who came to look at them at Nichols' farm. Brown made some of them for the neighboring farmers as well. But by 1983, Brown became engaged in the building of the new site. Though the building was subcontracted, Brown found himself spending full-time in negotiations with the building contractor because he was the only technical counterpart in the feed company.

Between 1980 and 1986, the company employed four new people in management positions.

Mr. Bunker, an agronomist, was employed to be in charge of production because William Nichols was not as familiar with it as his predecessor.

Mr. Faris, another agronomist, was called in as a marketing manager as the widening district of the clientele required more and more attention. In addition, agricultural exhibitions had become an important way of promoting the company. Mr. Faris took deliberate steps to increase sales to large wholesale companies instead of selling directly to the farmers. He also realized soon that Mr. Brown's devices looked like a promising business opportunity, and he began to develop the idea toward a new branch for the company.

Mr. Taft, also an agronomist, was hired as the superintendent of Nichol's family farm—one more job that nobody but a new man could take over from Michael Nichols. Taft established a little experimental laboratory to study the nutritional effects of different mixes of cattle feed.

Mr. Lindberg, a veterinary surgeon, was employed as a link between the company and the farmers; he traveled to the farmers' associations giving popular lectures on the nutrition of cattle.

The second generation of the Nichols family established themselves in the company quite well. Dennis had become a most effective salesman. John had developed purchasing to a key function of the company by keeping the costs at a low level—raw material made 70 percent of the costs of running the company. Sheila remained a bookkeeper, but after getting married and having children, she became less involved with the company.

William Nichols died in a traffic accident in 1988. The next day, Dennis Nichols was nominated as the general manager.

Dennis Nichols 1988-

Dennis Nichols had inherited a company that had a fairly good business base and a good reputation among the farmers. The farmers' devices turned out to be a growing business opportunity. Mr. Faris imported devices for farmers and discussed with Mr. Brown plans for establishing a manufacturing plant.

But there were also dark clouds on the horizon. The decreasing share of agriculture in the national economy and increasing competition from big companies were noticeable threats. The new plant would be ready within a year. It would be highly automatic; then, the labor costs would be reduced, but the heavy loans taken for the investment made capital costs higher.

Internal strains erupted quickly as Dennis Nichols commenced his new post. His former colleague Mr. McDougall, an effective salesman too, had an intense clash with Mr. Faris, the marketing manager. McDougall made it clear that either he would report directly to Dennis Nichols, or he would quit. Dennis Nichols agreed with McDougall's request as he did not want to lose an effective salesman. Nevertheless, the incompatibility of the self-made high-pressure salesman, Mr. McDougall, and the marketing strategist, Mr. Faris, caused daily friction.

Mr. Brown, the technical manager, and Mr. Bunker, the production manager, came to Dennis Nichols and requested that he define their duties. There were crucial functions in the new plant, and the men could not define the responsibilities themselves. Brown and

Bunker insisted that Nichols' definition of their duties would be necessary to guard against a foreseeable conflict. Bunker felt in charge of the continuous flow of production and Brown of service and maintenance—these two roles seemed to lead to irreconcilable views. Nichols did nothing but promised a more comprehensive survey of everyone's tasks, and on this occasion Brown's and Bunker's concerns would be settled.

Taft and Lindberg had developed a dispute about scientific leadership in the company. Taft claimed that Lindberg preached heresy to the farmers, while Lindberg doubted the scientific honesty of Taft's experiments that showed the superiority of his new mixture of cattle food.

Mr. Healy was again a most reliable subordinate of his new manager, and Dennis Nichols felt close to his competent controller. Mr. Healy had done his best for the company during three managers as a loyal servant of the family, but he had begun to feel an increasing animosity from other people in the company. He had reminded the agronomists now and then about cost factors and his advice had created friction.

John Nichols was absolutely loyal to his elder brother, but there seemed to be symptoms of difficulties between John Nichols and Mr. Healy.

Dennis's sister, Sheila Miles, also began to behave very critically toward Mr. Healy. In addition, she requested dividends of the company—during all these years she had received from the company just her salary as a bookkeeper, and now her growing family required more. Sheila also persuaded her mother to claim her dividends. Mr. Healy's accounts, on the other hand, showed to Dennis Nichols that paying back the investment in the new site and needed investments in the farmers' devices, in view of the likely decreasing possibilities in cattle feed production, would not leave much to divide during the years to come.

Dennis Nichols had inherited a company whose business base and image had been established and which had promised opportunities ahead. On the darker side, however, there were decreasing market possibilities for cattle feed, new financing difficulties of a family-owned investment-intensive company, and many personnel troubles. At the age of 28, Dennis Nichols faced the challenge of his life. He knew the company and its business quite thoroughly, but he had to grow from an effective salesman to a general manager of a middle-sized company. He was also fully aware that he had to show personnel that he is their general manager not only due to inheritance but due to managerial ability.

Discuss the Nichols Cattle Feed Company in a group. Prepare yourself for the discussion by reading the following instructions:

Instructions: In the case material, learning is based on the interaction of participants. To be able to do it, you must first read the case very carefully. The following points help you to prepare yourself for the discussion.

1. Familiarize yourself with the case. Get to know the facts, but try also to understand how the key persons feel in the situation.
2. After reading the case carefully, analyze it by paying attention to the following points:

    * the situation of the key persons as they see it
    * course, order, and timing of events
    * what is essential for decision making
    * try to develop alternative ways of proceeding from where the company stands
    * try to see potential obstacles of different, alternative decisions

3. Think about the case as a whole. Let ideas flow.
4. Remember that there is not one right solution to the case. While discussing the case in a group, do the following:

    * Present your views and be prepared to argue for them.
    * Listen to others and think about what they say.
    * Be open to new views and don't stick to your own views only.
    * Have fun!

Bibliography

Aaltio-Marjosola, I. (1991). Cultural change in a business enterprise: Studying a major organizational change and its impact on culture. Helsinki: Acta Academiae Oeconomicae Helsingiensis. Series A-80.

Adizes, I. (1979). *How to solve the mismanagement crisis.* Homewood, IL: Dow Jones-Irwin.

Adler, N. J. (1995). Competitive frontiers: Cross-cultural management and the 21st century. *International Journal of Intercultural Relations* 19(4): 523–537.

Ansoff, I., Declerck, P. P., and Hayes, R. L. (Eds.) (1976). *From strategic planning to strategic management.* Bruxelles: EIASM.

Arogyaswami, K., Barker, V. L., III, and Yasai-Adekani, M. (1995). Firm turnarounds: An integrative two-stage model. *Journal of Management Studies* 32(4): 493–525.

Ascari, A., Rock, M., and Dutta, S. (1995). Reengineering and organizational change: Lessions from a comparative analysis of company experiences. *European Management Journal* 13(1): 1–30.

Aupperle, K.E., Acar, W., and Booth, D. E. (1986). An empirical critique of in search of excellence: How excellent are the excellent companies? *Journal of Management,* 12(4): 499–512.

Baba, Y., and Imai, K-I. (1993). A network view of innovation and entrepreneurship: The case of the evolution of the VCR systems *International Social Science Journal* 35(1): 23–34.

Bales, R. F., and Slater, P. E. (1955). Role differentiation in small decision-making groups. In T. Parsons and Bales, R. F. in collaboration with Olds, J., Zelditch, M. Jr., and Slater, P. E. *The family, socialization, and interaction process.* (pp. 259–306). New York: The Free Press.

Barney, J. B., and Zajac, E. J. (1994). Competitive organizational behavior: Toward an organizationally based theory of competitive advantage. *Strategic Management Journal* 15:5–9. [Special issue: Competitive Organizational Behavior, J. B. Barney and E. Zajac (Eds.).]

Bassman, E., and London, M. (1993). Abusive managerial behavior. *Leadership and Organization Development Journal* 14(2): 18–24.

Becker, S. W. (1993). TQM does work: Ten reasons why misguided attempts fail. *Management Review* May: 30–36.

Bennis, W. (1989). Managing the dream: Leadership in the 21st century. *Journal of Organizational Change Management* 2: 6–10.

Bennis, W., and Nanus, B. (1985). *Leaders: The strategies for taking charge.* New York: Harper & Row.

Bettis, R. A., and Prahalad, C. K. (1995). The dominant logic: Retrospective and extension. *Strategic Management Journal* 16: 5–14.

Black, J. S., Mendenhall, M. E., and Oddou, G. (1991). Toward a comprehensive model of international adjustment: An integration of multiple theoretical perspectives. *Academy of Management Review* 16(2): 291–317.

Blake, R. R., and Mouton, J. S. (1964). *The managerial grid.* Houston: Gulf Publishing.

Blaney, G. (1966). *The tyranny of distance: How distance shaped Australia's history.* Melbourne: Sun Books.

Brett, J. M., and Stroh, L. K. (1995). Willingness to relocate internationally. *Human Resource Management* 34(3): 405–424.

Broms, H., and Gahmberg, H. (1979). Myths and language in strategic decisions. Paper presented in the workshop of strategic management practices. Saint-Maximin, France.

Burton, J. (1995). Composite strategy: The combination of collaboration and competition. *Journal of General Management* 21(1): 1–23.

Byrne, J. A. (1993). Requiem for yesterday's CEO: Old-style execs who can't adapt are losing their hold. *Business Week* (February, 15): 28–29.

Cadbury, A. (1987). Ethical managers make their own rules. *Harvard Business Review* (September-October): 69–73.

Calas, M., and Smircich, L. (1993). Dangerous liaisons: The "feminine-in-management" meets "globalization." *Business Horizons* (March-April): 71–80.

Campbell, A., Goold, M., and Alexander, M. (1995). The value of the parent company. *California Management Review* 31(1): 79–97.

Carlson, S. (1951). *Executive behaviour: A study of the work load and the working methods of managing directors.* Stockholm: Strömbergs.

Churchman, C. W. (1977). *The systems approach.* New York: Dell.

Clarke, C., and Hammer, M. R. (1995). Predictions of Japanese and American managers' job success, personal adjustment, and intercultural interaction effectiveness. *Management International Review* 35(2): 153–170.

Coates, J. F., and Jarratt, T. (1989). *What futurists believe.* A world future society book. Mt. Airy, MD: Lomon.

Conger, J. A., and Kanungo, R.N. (1988). Introduction: Problems and prospects in understanding charismatic leadership. In J. A. Conger and R. N. Kanungo (Eds.) *Charismatic leadership: Elusive factor in organizational effectiveness.* San Francisco: Jossey-Bass, pp. 637–647.

Cummings, S. (1995). Pericles of Athens—Drawing from the essence of strategic leadership. *Business Horizons* 38(1): 22–27.

Dahrendorf, R. (1959). *Class and class conflict in industrial society.* Stanford, CA: Stanford University Press.

Darling, J. R. (1991). Improving communication in organizational leadership: Effective use of the social style model. *Psychology* 28(2): 1–14.

Darling, J. R. (1992). Total quality management: The key role of leadership strategies. *Leadership and Organizational Development Journal* 13(4): 3–7.

Darling, J. R. (1994). Crisis management in international business: Keys to effective decision making. *Leadership and Organization Development Journal* 15(8): 3–8.

Darling, J. R., and Cornesky, R. A. (1987). Keys to conflict management and leadership. *Leadership and Organization Development Journal* 8(1): i-vi.

Darling, J. R., and Nurmi, R. (1995). Downsizing the multinational firm: Key variables for excellence. *Leadership and Organization Development Journal* 16(5): 22–28.

Darling, J. R., and Taylor, R. E. (1986). Upward management: Getting in step with the boss. *Business* 36(2): 3–8.

Darling, J. R., and Taylor, R. E. (1989). A model for reducing resistance to change in a firm's international marketing strategy. *European Journal of Marketing* 23(7): 34–41.

Davidow, W. H., and Malone, M. S. (1992). *The virtual corporation. Lessons from the world's most advanced companies. Structuring and revitalizing the corporation for the 21st century.* New York: Harper Business.

Deal, T. E., and Kennedy, A.A. (1982). *Corporate cultures. The rites and rituals of corporate life.* Reading, PA: Addison-Wesley.

Delacroix, J., and Saudagaran, S. M. (1991). Munificent compensation as disincentives: The case of American CEOs. *Human Relations* 44(7): 665–678.

Deming, W. E. (1986). *Out of the crisis.* Cambridge: The MIT Press.

Denison, D. R. (1985). *Corporate culture and organizational effectiveness.* New York: Wiley.

Dennison, R. N., Hooijberg, R., and Quinn, R. E. (1995). Paradox and performance: Toward a theory of behavioral complexity in managerial leadership. *Organization Science* 6(5) (September-October): 524–540.

DePree, M. (1987). *Leadership is an art.* East Lansing, MI: Michigan State University Press.

Dodgson, M. (1993). Organizational Learning: A review of some literature. *Organization Studies* 14(3): 375–394.

Drucker, P. F. (1954). *The practice of management.* New York: Harper and Row.

Earley, P., and Singh, H. S. (1995). International and intercultural management research: What's next? *Academy of Management Journal* 38(2): 327–340.

Exodus. The Second Book of Moses. *The Holy Bible.* Authorized King James Version. London: Collins' Clear-type Press.

Fairburn, J., and Geroski, P. (1989). The Empirical Analysis of Market Structure and Performance. In J. A. Fairburn and J. A. Kay (Eds.). *Mergers and merger policy.* Oxford: Oxford University Press, pp. 175–192.

Fayol, H. (1949). *General and industrial management.* New York: Pitman.

Ford, D. G., and Harris, J. J., III (1992). The elusive definition of creativity. *Journal of Creative Behavior* 26(3): 186–198.

Ford, J. N., and Ford, L. W. (1995). The role of conversations in producing intentional change in organizations. *Academy of Management Review* 20(3): 541–570.

Gahmberg, H. (1986). *Symbols and values of strategic managers: A semiotic approach.* Helsinki: Acta Academiae Oeconomiae Helsingiensis. Series A-47.

George, C. S., Jr. (1972). *The history of management thought.* Englewood Cliffs, NJ: Prentice-Hall.

Ghiselli, E. E. (1971). *Explorations in managerial talent.* Pacific Palisades, CA: Goodyear.

Goddard, J., and Houlder, D. (1995). Beyond magic: Conjectures on the nature of strategy in the late 1990s. *Business Strategy Review* 1(1) (Spring): 81–107.

Goold, M., and Campbell, A. (1987). *Strategies and styles: The role of the center in managing diversified corporations.* Oxford: Basil Blackwell.

Grandori, A., and Soda, G. (1995). Inter-firm networks, antecedants, mechanisms, and forms. *Organization Studies* 16(2): 183–214.

Grönhaug, K., and Falkenberg, J. (1990). Organizational success and success criteria: Conceptual issues and an empirical illustration. *Scandinavian Journal of Management* 6(4): 267–284.

Grönroos, C. (1990). *Service management and marketing.* Lexington, MA: Lexington Books.

Gupta, A. K., and Govindarajan, V. (1984). Business unit strategy, management characteristics, and business unit effectiveness at strategy implementation. *Academy of Management Journal* 27(1): 25–41.

Hahn, D. (1991). Strategic management: Tasks and challenges in the 1990s. *Long Range Planning* 24(1): 26–39.

Hamblin, R. L. (1958). Leadership and crises. *Sociometry* 21: 322–335.

Hamel, G. and Prahalad, C. K. (1993). Strategy as strength and leverage. *Harvard Business Review* (March-April): 75–84.

Hampden-Turner, C. (1990). *Corporate culture: From vicious to virtuous circles.* London: Economist Books.

Handscombe, R., and Norman, R. (1989). *Strategic leadership: The missing links.* London: McGraw-Hill.

Hannan, M. T., and Freeman, J. (1989). *Organizational ecology.* Cambridge, MA: Harvard University Press.

Harari, O. (1993). The eleventh reason why TGM doesn't work. *Management Review* (May): 31–36.

Harju, P. (1981). *Attitude of strategic managers toward formalized corporate planning.* Turku, Finland: Publications of the Turku School of Economics. Series A-1.

Harrington, H. J. (1991). *Business process in improvement.* New York: McGraw-Hill.

Harris, P. R., and Moran, R. T. (1987). *Managing cultural differences: High-performance strategies for today's global manager.* Houston: Gulf Publishing.

Havas, J. (1993). *The correlation of the result of a campaign with some leadership and organizational variables.* Unpublished manuscript.

Hedley, B. (1977). Strategy and business portfolio. *Long Range Planning* 10: 2.

Heller, J. E. (1980). Criteria for selecting an international manager. *Personnel* (May-June): 47–55.

Herzberg, F., Mausner, B., and Snyderman, B. B. (1959). *The motivation to work.* New York: Wiley.

Hodgetts, R. M., and Luthans, F. (1991). *International management.* New York: McGraw-Hill.

Hofstede, G. H. (1967). *The game of budget control.* London: Tavistock.

Hofstede, G. (1980). *Culture's consequences: International differences in work-related values.* Beverly Hills: Sage.

House, R. J., and Baetz, M. L. (1979). Leadership: Some empirical generalizations and new research directions. In B. M. Staw (Ed.). *Research in Organizational Behavior,* volume 1 (pp. 348–354). Greenwich, CT: JAI Press.

Humble, J. W. (1968). *Improving business results.* Maidenhead, England: McGraw-Hill.

Huse, E. F. (1989). *Organization development and change,* fourth edition. St. Paul, MN: West Publishing Company.

Iacocca, L. (1984). *Iacocca: An autobiography.* New York: Bantam Books.

Janis, I. L. (1972). *Victims of groupthink*. Boston: Houghton Mifflin.

Javidan, M. (1991). Leading a high-commitment high-performance organization. *Long Range Planning* 24(2): 28–36.

Jehn, K. A. (1995). A multimethod examination of the benefits and detriments of intragroup conflict. *Administrative Science Quarterly* 40: 256–282.

Johnson, G., and Scholes, K. (1993). *Exploring corporate strategy: Text and cases,* third edition. London: Prentice-Hall.

Kapoor, A., Hansén, S-O, and Davidson, R. (1991). *Negotiating internationally: The Art of networking*. Hanko, Finland: Recalmed.

Katz, D., and Kahn, R. L. (1966). *The social psychology of organizations*. New York: Wiley.

Katz, D., Maccoby, N., and Morse, N. (1950). *Productivity, supervision, and morale in an office situation*. Ann Arbor: The Michigan Survey Research Center.

Kauppinen, M. (1994). Antecedants of expatriate adjustment: An integration of multiple theoretical perspectives. *Acta Universitatis Oeconomiae Helsingiensis*. B-140.

Knoke, D., and Kuklinski, J. H. (1982). *Network analysis*. Beverly Hills: Sage.

Koontz, H. (1961). The management theory jungle. *Academy of Management Journal* 4: 174–188.

Koontz, H. (1980). The management theory jungle revisited. *Academy of Management Review* 5(2): 175–187.

Kotter, J. P. (1988). *The leadership factor*. New York: Free Press.

Kreiner, K., and Schultz, M. (1993). Informal collaboration in R and D: The formation of networks across organizations. *Organization Studies* 14(2): 189–209.

Kulisch, T., and Banner, D. K. (1993). Self-managed work-teams: An update. *Leadership and Organization Development Journal* 14(2): 25–29.

Lähteenmäki, S. (1993). Individual coping patterns in career behaviour: Sources of personnel risks or possibilities for better human resource management? A paper presented at the 8th Workshop on Strategic HRM in Toronto.

Lähteenmäki, S., and Paalumäki, A. (1993). The retraining and mobility motivations of key personnel: Dependencies in the

Finnish business environment. *The International Journal of Human Resource Management* 4(2): 377–406.

Lao, Tzu. *The Tao Te Ching.* Trans. S. Mitchell. *Exploring Ancient World Cultures: Readings from Ancient China.* Online. Available: http://eawe.evansville.edu/anthology/tao.htm.

Larsson, R. (1990). *Coordination of action in mergers and acquisitions.* Lund, Sweden: Lund University Press.

Laughlin, R. C. (1991). Environmental disturbances and organizational transitions and transformations: Some alternative models. *Organization Studies* 12(2): 209–232.

Lehtimäki, J. (1993). *Towards a theory of the university as a knowledge-intensive organization.* Turku, Finland Publications of the Turku School of Economics and Business Administration. Series A-5.

Lehtimäki, J., Kontkanen, L. and Nurmi, R. (1991). An organization theoretical framework of knowledge organizations. *Administrative Studies* 1: 41–49.

Lenz, R. T., and Lyles, M. A. (1985). Paralysis by analysis: Is your planning system becoming too rational? *Long Range Planning* 18(4): 64–72.

Lewin, K. (1935). *A dynamic theory of personality.* New York: McGraw-Hill.

Lewin, K. (1948). Problems in changing culture. In G. L. Lewin (Ed.): *Resolving social conflicts: Selected papers on group dynamics.* (pp. 1–68). New York: Harper and Row.

Likert, R. (1961). *New patterns of management.* New York: McGraw-Hill.

Lipshitz, R., and Nevo, B. (1992) Who is a "good manager"? *Leadership and Organization Development Journal* 13(6): 3–7.

Liuhto, K. (1991). *The interaction of managerial cultures in the Soviet-Finnish joint ventures. Including Estonian-Finnish joint ventures.* Monograph. Turku, Finland: Institute for East-West Trade. Publications of the Turku School of Economics and Business Administration.

Lumijärvi, O-P. (1990). *Gameplaying in capital budgeting.* Turku, Finland: Publications of the Turku School of Economics. Series A-7.

Magnusen, K. O. (1995). The legacy of leadership revisited. *Business Horizons* 38(6): 3–7.

Mamman, A. (1995). Socio-biographical antecedants of intercultural effectiveness: The neglected factors. *British Journal of Management* (6): 97–144.

Markides, C., and Stopford, J. M. (1995). From ugly ducklings to elegant swans: Transforming parochial firms into world leaders. *Business Strategy Review* 6(2) (Winter): 1–24.

Maslow, A. H. (1954). *Motivation and personality.* New York: Harper & Row.

May, D. R., and Flannery, B. L. (1995). Cutting waste with employee involvement teams. *Business Horizons* 38(5): 28–38.

McFarland, D. E. (1974). *Management: Foundations and practices,* fifth edition. New York: Macmillan.

McGregor, D. (1960). *The human side of enterprise.* New York: McGraw-Hill.

McGregor, D. (1967). *The professional manager.* London: McGraw-Hill.

McGuinness, T. (1991). Markets and managerial hierarchies. In G. Thompson, J. Frances, R. Levacic, and J. Mitchell (Eds.). *Markets, hierarchies, and networks: The Coordination of social life.* (66–81). London: Sage.

Megginson, L. C., Mosley, D. C., and Pietri, P. H., Jr. (1992). *Management: Concepts and applications,* fourth edition. New York: HarperCollins.

Mendenhall, M., and Oddou, G. (1986). Acculturation profiles of expatriate managers: Implications for cross-cultural training programs. *Columbia Journal of World Business* 2(14): 73–79.

Milestones in the management game over four decades. (1986). *International Management* (August): 26–27. [Special 40th Anniversary Issue.]

Miller, D., Kets de Vries, M. F. R., and Toulouse, J. M. (1982). Top executive locus of control and its relationship to strategy-making, structure, and environment. *Academy of Management Journal* 25: 237–253.

Mintzberg, H. (1973). *The nature of managerial work.* New York: Harper & Row.

Mintzberg, H. (1987). The strategy concept I: Five Ps for strategy. *California Management Review* 30(1): 11– 24.

Mintzberg, H., and Waters, J. A. (1985). Of strategies, deliberate and emergent. *Strategic Management Journal* 6(3) 257–272.

Moorhead, G., Ference, R., and Neck, C. P. (1991). Group decision fiascoes continue: Space shuttle Challenger and a revised group-think framework. *Human Relations* 44(6): 539–550.

Murnighan, J. K., and Conlon, D. E. (1991). The dynamics of intense work groups: A study of British string quartets. *Administrative Science Quarterly* 36: 165–186.

Naisbitt, J., and Aburdene, P. (1990). *Megatrends 2000: Ten new, directions for the 1990's.* New York: Warner Books.

Nonaka, I. (1991). The knowledge-creating company. *Harvard Business Review* 69: 96–104.

Noon, M., and Delbridge, R. (1993). News from behind my hand: Gossip in organizations. *Organization Studies* 14: 23–36.

Nurmi, R. (1976). Developing a climate for planning. *Long Range Planning* (June): 48–53.

Nurmi, R. (1983). *Esimiestyön Luonne. Erään Teorian Tarkastelua.* With an English summary: A discussion on a management theory with Finnish CEOs. Turku, Finland: Publications of the Turku School of Economics. A-5.

Nurmi, R. (1984). Aristotle and management. *Scandinavian Journal of Management* 1: 65–73.

Nurmi, R. (1986). *A cross-cultural note on Australian and Finnish values.* Occasional paper 94. Geelong, Australia: Deakin University, School of Management.

Nurmi, R. (1987). *Minkälainen on Tehokas Johtaja?* With an English summary: What makes an effective manager? Publications of the Turku School of Economics. A-4.

Nurmi, R. (1990). Management in Finland. *European Management Journal* 8(1): 96–104.

Nurmi, R. (1992). Corporate transformation: A Scandinavian example of a "middle of the road" approach. *Leadership and Organization Development Journal* 13(5): i–vi.

Nurmi, R., Kontkanen, L., Lehtimäki, J., and Viitanen, P. (1992). Knowledge organizations: A typological and a structural note. *The Finnish Journal of Business Economics* (1): 13–20.

Nurmi, R., and Udo-aka, U. (1980). Management research for management development in a developing country: A model and a case. *Management International Review* (20): 90–95.

Nurmi, R., and Üksvärav, R. (1993). How Estonian managers experienced the transformation to independence and market economy in 1990–1991. *Management International Review* 33: 171–181.

Näsi, J. (Ed.) (1991a). *Arenas of strategic thinking*. Helsinki: Foundation of Economic Education.

Näsi, J. (1991b). Strategic thinking as doctrine: Development of focus areas and new insights. In J. Näsi (Ed.) *Arenas of strategic thinking*. (pp. 26–64). Helsinki: Foundation of Economic Education.

Odiorne, G., Weinrich, H., and Mendleson, J. (1980). *Executive skills: A management by objectives approach*. Dubuque, IA: WCH.

Ohmae, K. (1982). *The mind of the strategist: The art of Japanese business*. New York: McGraw-Hill.

O'Toole, J. (1985). *Vanguard management: Redesigning the corporate future*. New York: Doubleday and Company, Inc.

Ouchi, W. G. (1980). Markets, bureaucracies, and clans. *Administrative Science Quarterly* 25: 12–141.

Pastin, M. (1986). *The hard problems of management: Gaining the ethics edge*. San Francisco: Jossey-Bass.

Peters, T., and Austin, N. (1985). *A passion for excellence*. New York: Random House.

Peters, T., and Waterman, R. H., Jr. (1982). *In search of excellence: Lessons from America's best-run companies*. New York: Harper & Row.

Pfeffer, J., and Salancik, G. R. (1978). *The external control of organizations: A resource dependence perspective*. New York: Harper & Row.

Phatak, A. V. (1989). *International dimensions of management*, second edition. Boston: PWS-Kent.

Pinchot, C. III. (1985). *Intrapreneuring*. New York: Harper and Row.

Polanyi, M. (1962). *Personal knowledge: Towards a post-critical philosophy*. New York: Harper & Row.

Porter, M. (1980). *Competitive strategy*. New York: The Free Press.

Porter, M. (1985). *Competitive advantage: Creating and sustaining superior performance*. New York: The Free Press.

Porter, L. W., and Lawler, E. E. (1968). *Managerial attitudes and performance.* Homewood, AL: Irwin.

Potts, M., and Behr, D. (1987). *The leading edge: CEOs who turned their companies around. What they did and how they did it.* New York: McGraw-Hill.

Powell, W. W. (1990). Neither market nor hierarchy: Network forms of organization. *Research in Organizational Behavior* 12: 295–336.

Prahalad, C. K., and Hamel, G. (1990). The core competence of the corporation. *Harvard Business Review* (May-June): 79–91.

Quinn, R. E., and Cameron, K. S. (1988). Paradox and transformation: A dynamic theory of organization and management. In R. E. Quinn and K. S. Cameron (Eds.). *Paradox and transformation: Toward a theory of change and management.* (pp. 289–308). Cambridge, MA: Ballinger.

Reddin, W. J. (1970). *Managerial effectiveness.* New York: McGraw-Hill.

Reddin, W. J. (1971). *Effective management by objectives: The 3-D method of MBO.* New York: McGraw-Hill.

Reve, T. (1990). The firm as a nexus of internal and external contracts. In: M. Aoki, B. Gustafsson, and O. E. Williamson (Eds.). *The firm as a nexus of treaties.* (pp. 133–161). London: Sage.

Rhenman, E. (1973). *Organizations theory for long range planning.* London: Wiley.

Roddick, A. (1991). *Body and soul, profits and principles—The amazing success story of Anita Roddick of The Body Shop.* New York: Crown Publishers.

Ronen, S. (1986). *Corporate and multinational management.* New York: Wiley.

Ropo, A. (1989). *Leadership and organizational change.* Tampere, Finland: Acta Universitatis Tamperensis. A-280.

Rubin, P. H. (1990) *Managing business transactions: Controlling the costs of coordinating, communicating, and decision making.* New York: The Free Press.

Sagers, M., and Johnson, A. (1991). Viel vorschuss für baltentroika, wenig hoffnung für asiatischen provinzen. *Plan Econ. Manager Magazine* 10: 32–33.

Santalainen, T. J., and Hunt, J. G. (1988). Change differences from an action research, results-oriented OD program in high- and low-performing Finnish banks. *Group and Organization Studies* 13: 413–440.

Sarbin, T. R., and Allen, V. L. (1968). Role theory. In G. Lindzey and E. Aronson (Eds.). *The handbook of social psychology,* volume 1. (pp. 488–567). Reading, PA: Addison Wesley.

Schein, E. H. (1985). *Organizational culture and leadership.* San Francisco: Jossey-Bass.

Schendel, D. (ed.) (1989). On strategic leadership. *Strategic Management Journal* 10: 1–3. [Second special issue.]

Schneider, J., and Locke, E. A. (1971). A critique of Herzberg's incident classification system and a suggested revision. *Organizational Behavior and Human Performance* 6: 441–457.

Schoeffler, S. (1980). *Nine basic findings of business strategy. The Pims letters on business strategy 1.* Boston: The Strategic Planning Institute.

Schreyögg, G. (1980). Contingency and choice in organization theory. *Organization Studies* 1: 305–326.

Sherman, S. P. (1989). Inside the mind of Jack Welch. *Fortune* March 27, 39.

Sitkin, S. B., and Bies, R. J. (1993). Social accounts in conflict situations: Using explanations to manage conflicts. *Human Relations* 46: 349–370.

Slater, S. F. (1995). Learning to change. *Business Horizons* 38(6): 13–20.

Slatter, S. (1984). *Corporate recovery: A guide to turnaround management.* Harmondsworth, England: Penguin 1986.

Sloan, A. P., Jr. (1972). *My years with General Motors.* New York: Anchor Books.

Smircich, L. (1983). Concepts of culture and organizational analysis. *Administrative Science Quarterly* 28: 339–358.

Smith, C. and Gemmil, G. (1991). Change in the small group: A dissipative structure perspective. *Human Relations* 44(7): 69–716.

Snow, C. E., Miles, R. E., and Coleman, H. J., Jr. (1992). Managing 21st century network organizations. *Organizational Dynamics* (Winter): 5–19.

Sooklal, L. (1991). The leader as a broker of dreams. *Human Relations* 44(8): 833–856.

Spendolini, M. J. (1992). *The benchmarking book.* New York: Amacom.

Stacey, R. N. (1995). The science of complexity: An alternative perspective for strategic change process. *Strategic Management Journal* 16: 477–495.

Staw, B. M., and Barsade, S. G. (1993). Affect and managerial performance: A test of the sadder-but-wiser vs. happier-and-smarter hypotheses. *Administrative Science Quarterly* 38: 304–331.

Stumpf, S. A., and Muellen, T. P. (1991). Strategic leadership: Concepts, skill, style, and process. *Journal of Management Development* 10(1): 42–53.

Suomi, R. (1990). *Assessing the feasibility of interorganizational information systems on the basis of the transaction cost approach.* Turku, Finland: Publications of the Turku School of Economics and Business Administration. A-3.

Sveiby, K. E., and Lloyd, T. (1987). *Managing knowhow.* London: Bloomsbury.

Sweeney, P. J., and Allen, D. M. (1984). Teams which excel. *Research Management* 1: 19–22.

Taylor, F. W. (1903). Shop management. In H. S. Person (Ed.): *Scientific management.* (pp. 1–207). (1964). New York: Harper & Row.

Taylor, F. W. (1911). The principles of scientific management. In H. S. Person (Ed.): *Scientific Management.* (1964). New York: Harper & Row.

Taylor's testimony before the special house committee (1912). A reprint of the public document. In H. S. Person (Ed.): *Scientific management.* (1964). New York: Harper & Row.

Taylor, W. (1993). Message and muscle: An interview with Swatch Titan Nicolas Hayek. *Harvard Business Review* (March-April): 99–110.

Thomas, A. B. (1988). Does leadership make a difference to organizational performance? *Administrative Science Quarterly* 33: 388–400.

Thornton, R. L., and Thornton, M. K. (1995). Personnel problems in "carry the flag" missions in foreign assignments. *Business Horizons* 38(1): 59–66.

Timm, P. R., Peterson, P. D., and Stevens, J. C. (1990). *People at work: Human relations in organizations,* third edition. St. Paul, MN: West Publishing Company.

Toffler, A. (1990). *Powershift: Knowledge, wealth, and violence at the edge of 21st century.* New York: Bantam.

Tomasko, R. M. (1987). *Downsizing: Reshaping the corporation for the future.* New York: Amacom.

Tung, R. L. (1982). Selection and training procedures of U.S., European, and Japanese multinationals. *California Management Review* (Fall): 59.

Tung, R. L. (1986). Corporate executives and their families in China: The need for cross-cultural understanding in business. *Columbia Journal of World Business* 21(1) (Spring): 21–25.

Tung, R. L. (1987). Expatriate assignments: Enhancing success and minimizing failure. *Academy of Management Executive* (May): 117.

Üksvärav, R. (1991). From planned to market economy: The Estonian case. *Business in the Contemporary World* (Summer): 63–70.

Üksvärav, R., and Nurmi, R. (1993). *Estonian economy and management in the early 1990s.* Turku, Finland: Publications of the Turku School of Economics and Business Administration. Series A-4.

Viitanen, P. (1993). *Strategian muotoutumisprosessi ja strategiset muutokset tietointensiivisessä organisaatiossa.* With an English summary: The process of strategy formation and strategic change in a knowledge-intensive organization. Turku, Finland: Publications of the Turku School of Economics and Business Administration. Series D-2.

Vroom, V. H. (1964). *Work and motivation.* New York: Wiley.

Wagner, C. K. (1995). Managing change in business: Views from the ancient past. *Business Horizons* 38(6): 8–12.

Waldersee, R., and Sheather, S. (1996). The effects of strategy type on strategy implementation actions. *Human Relations* 49(1): 105–122.

Weber, M. (1978). *Economy and society.* G. Roth and C. Wittich (Eds.). Berkeley: University of California Press.

Weick, K. E. (1976). Educational organizations as loosely coupled systems. *Administrative Science Quarterly* 21: 1–19.

Weick, K. E. (1979). *The social psychology of organizing.* New York: Random House.

Wernerfelt, B. (1995). The resource-based view of the firm: Ten years after. *Strategic Management Journal* 16: 171–174.

White, R. F., and Jacques, R. (1995). Operationalizing the postmodernity construct for efficient organizational change management. *Journal of Organizational Change Management* 8(2): 45–71.

Wick, C. W., and Leon, L. S. (1995). From ideas to action: Creating a learning organization. *Human Resource Management* 34(2): 299–311.

Williamson, O. E. (1991). Comparative economic organization: The analysis of discrete structural alternatives. *Administrative Science Quarterly* 36: 269–296.

Woodward, J. (1965). *Industrial organization: Theory and practice.* Oxford: Oxford University Press.

Yukl, G. A. (1989). *Leadership in organizations.* Englewood Cliffs, NJ: Prentice-Hall.

Zaheer, S. (1995). Overcoming the liability of foreigners. *Academy of Management Journal* 38(2): 341–363.

Zeira, Y., and Banai, M. (1985). Selection of expatriate managers in MNCs: The host-environment point of view. *International Studies of Management and Organization* (Spring): 33–51.

Zilbert, E. R. (1991). Management in the 1990s? *Journal of Management Development* 10(2): 7–14.

Index

Page numbers followed by the letter "f" indicate figures.

Order Your Own Copy of This Important Book for Your Personal Library!

INTERNATIONAL MANAGEMENT LEADERSHIP
The Primary Competitive Advantage

_____ in hardbound at $49.95 (ISBN: 0-7890-0090-3)

_____ in softbound at $24.95 (ISBN: 0-7890-0260-4)

COST OF BOOKS_____	☐ **BILL ME LATER:** ($5 service charge will be added) (Bill-me option is good on US/Canada/Mexico orders only; not good to jobbers, wholesalers, or subscription agencies.)
OUTSIDE USA/CANADA/ MEXICO: ADD 20%_____	
POSTAGE & HANDLING_____ *(US: $3.00 for first book & $1.25 for each additional book) Outside US: $4.75 for first book & $1.75 for each additional book)*	☐ Check here if billing address is different from shipping address and attach purchase order and billing address information. Signature_____
SUBTOTAL_____	☐ **PAYMENT ENCLOSED: $**_____
IN CANADA: ADD 7% GST_____	☐ **PLEASE CHARGE TO MY CREDIT CARD.**
STATE TAX_____ *(NY, OH & MN residents, please add appropriate local sales tax)*	☐ Visa ☐ MasterCard ☐ AmEx ☐ Discover ☐ Diners Club Account # _____
FINAL TOTAL_____ *(If paying in Canadian funds, convert using the current exchange rate. UNESCO coupons welcome.)*	Exp. Date _____ Signature _____

Prices in US dollars and subject to change without notice.

NAME _____

INSTITUTION _____

ADDRESS _____

CITY _____

STATE/ZIP _____

COUNTRY _____ COUNTY (NY residents only) _____

TEL _____ FAX _____

E-MAIL_____
May we use your e-mail address for confirmations and other types of information? ☐ Yes   ☐ No

Order From Your Local Bookstore or Directly From
The Haworth Press, Inc.
10 Alice Street, Binghamton, New York 13904-1580 • USA
TELEPHONE: 1-800-HAWORTH (1-800-429-6784) / Outside US/Canada: (607) 722-5857
FAX: 1-800-895-0582 / Outside US/Canada: (607) 772-6362
E-mail: getinfo@haworth.com
PLEASE PHOTOCOPY THIS FORM FOR YOUR PERSONAL USE.

BOF96